THE ARTIST'S GUIDE TO AI

TOOLS, STRATEGIES, AND ETHICS FOR THE MODERN CREATIVE

ARDEN VALE

CONTENTS

INTRODUCTION

In a small art studio in Brooklyn, a graphic designer named Lila stares at her computer screen, feeling stuck. She's been tasked with creating a new logo for a client, but the ideas just aren't flowing. Suddenly, her screen flashes with a message: "Need some inspiration? Try our new AI-powered design tool." Intrigued, Lila clicks the link and watches in awe as the AI generates dozens of unique logo concepts in seconds. With a few tweaks and her own creative touch, Lila has a winning design that her client loves. This is just one example of how AI is transforming the creative landscape, and it's only the beginning.

Welcome to "The Artist's Guide to AI: Tools, Strategies, and Ethics for the Modern Creative" As an artist and designer, I've witnessed firsthand the incredible potential of AI to revolutionize how we create. This book is your comprehensive guide to harnessing that power and seamlessly integrating AI into your creative process.

My vision for this book is simple: to empower you with practical, actionable insights that you can implement immediately. Each chapter is designed to build your knowledge and skills, culminating in a toolkit of AI-powered techniques that will elevate your work and keep you at the forefront of your field.

The numbers don't lie: AI is already making waves in the creative industry. A recent survey found that 75% of artists and designers believe AI will significantly impact their work within the next five years. The possibilities are endless, from AI-generated music indistinguishable from human compositions to AI-assisted writing tools that can craft compelling stories.

Whether you're a graphic designer, illustrator, musician, or writer, this book is for you. As a beginner, you'll find clear explanations and step-by-step guides that demystify AI and make it accessible. More experienced creatives will discover advanced techniques and thought-provoking case studies that push the boundaries of what's possible.

So, what sets this book apart? "The Artist's Guide to AI Prompting" is not just another theoretical exploration of AI in the arts. It's a hands-on, practical guide focusing on real-world applications and results. You'll find a wealth of examples, tutorials, and exercises that you can immediately put into practice.

But this book is about more than just technical skills. It's about embracing a new mindset that sees AI not as a threat but as a collaborator and creative catalyst. As someone who has navigated this transition, I'll share my journey and the lessons I've learned.

In the coming chapters, we'll cover everything from the basics of AI to the latest tools and techniques. You'll learn to use AI to generate ideas, streamline your workflow, and push your creative boundaries. We'll also explore the ethical considerations surrounding AI and creativity, ensuring you can use these tools responsibly and effectively.

By the end of this book, you'll have a robust understanding of AI and its creative applications. You'll be armed with practical techniques and a roadmap for continuous learning and growth. Most importantly, you'll be ready to face the future of creativity with confidence and excitement.

So, let's dive in. Whether you're a curious beginner or a seasoned pro, "The Artist's Guide to AI Prompting" is your key to unlocking AI's full potential in your creative work. Together, we'll explore the frontiers of this exciting new world and discover what's possible when human creativity meets artificial intelligence. Turn the page, and let's get started!

1 THE TRANSFORMATIVE POWER OF AI IN ART

Some years ago, a peculiar art exhibit in London captured the attention of critics and casual onlookers alike. The exhibit featured a series of paintings, each with vivid colours and abstract shapes, reminiscent of the works of Kandinsky. Yet, these were not the creations of a human artist. Instead, they were borne from the mind of a machine, a neural network trained to paint in the style of the great masters. This event marked a significant milestone in the art world: the rise of AI as a formidable force in creative endeavours. The exhibit proved one thing: machines could not only mimic human creativity but also inspire it. It was a wake-up call for artists everywhere, signalling an era of boundless possibilities and a shift in how we define creativity itself.

Welcome to the first chapter of "The Creatives Guide to AI Prompting: How to Future-proof Your Work and Turbocharge Your Career." Here, we explore how artificial intelligence is reshaping the very fabric of creativity. This isn't just about machines taking over the canvas; it's about redefining what it means to be an artist in the digital age. As we delve into the transformative potential of AI, you'll gain insights into how these technologies are broadening creative horizons. You'll discover AI's ability to push beyond the limits of traditional methods, offering new techniques and mediums that were once unimaginable.

1.1 REDEFINING CREATIVITY WITH AI

AI is challenging the status quo by introducing generative art algorithms capable of crafting unique art pieces. Much like the iconic AARON software developed by Harold Cohen, these algorithms function as autonomous creators, producing intricate designs without human intervention. They offer artists new exploration tools, from abstract digital landscapes to algorithmically generated sculptures. This isn't just about creating art but providing a new playground where creativity knows no bounds. Artists like Refik Anadol and Mario Klingemann are already pushing these boundaries, using AI to produce works that redefine what digital art can be. Their contributions highlight a pivotal shift: AI isn't just a tool—it's an active participant in the creative process.

The music industry, too, has not been immune to AI's influence. AI-assisted music composition tools have emerged as indispensable allies for composers seeking to develop complex scores with minimal effort. These tools, such as AIVA and Melodrive, use sophisticated algorithms to generate rich, emotionally resonant compositions that rival human-created music. They're not just making noise; they're crafting symphonies. Whether scoring a film, designing a video game soundtrack, or simply composing for pleasure, AI offers a new dimension of creativity that streamlines the process without compromising quality. As AI continues to evolve, so does its ability to enhance and inspire musical innovation, providing composers with a partner that understands the intricacies of sound and emotion.

AI's role extends beyond mere creation; it actively expands the boundaries of artistic expression. Techniques like Deep Dream and neural style transfer allow artists to blend styles and generate surreal imagery that defies traditional conventions. Deep Dream, pioneered by Google, uses neural networks to enhance image patterns, creating dream-like visuals that captivate and challenge perceptions. Meanwhile, neural style transfer combines one image's content with another's style, resulting in both novel and familiar artwork. These tools are not just technological marvels but catalysts for a new wave of artistic exploration, enabling creators to venture into realms that were once the stuff of imagination.

The advent of AI in art also prompts us to reconsider the very definition of an artist. No longer bound by the limitations of manual creation, artists now have the opportunity to collaborate with AI, treating it as a creative partner rather than a mere tool. This partnership allows for exploring new ideas, techniques, and mediums, broadening the scope of what art can be. AI's capacity to analyze vast amounts of data and generate insights offers artists a unique perspective that can inform and elevate their work. As we embrace this new era, the line between human and machine creativity blurs, challenging us to rethink what it means to be an artist.

Virtual reality (VR) environments powered by AI exemplify this shift by offering immersive and interactive art experiences that engage audiences in unprecedented ways. VR transforms art from a passive observation into an active exploration, where viewers can step inside a painting or interact with digital sculptures. AI's role in creating these environments is crucial, as it allows for real-time adaptations that respond to viewer input, making each experience unique and personal. This convergence of AI and VR represents a new frontier in artistic expression, where the boundaries between creator and audience dissolve, and art becomes a shared journey of discovery and innovation.

Reflection Section: Exploring Your Creative
Horizons with AI

Consider how AI might influence your artistic
practice. Reflect on the following questions:

1. How might generative algorithms inspire new
directions in your work?

2. Can AI-assisted tools streamline parts of
your creative process?

3. What are the potential challenges and
opportunities of collaborating with AI as a
creative partner?

Use these reflections to identify areas where AI
might enhance or challenge your current
creative practices and consider how you might
integrate these technologies into your work.

1.2 AI AS A CREATIVE COLLABORATOR

In the vibrant tapestry of today's art world, AI emerges as a companion rather than a competitor. The synergy between AI and human creativity is akin to a well-rehearsed duet, where each partner's strengths enhance the other's. Take, for example, the collaborative painting projects where artists and AI algorithms co-create. Human intuition meets machine precision, resulting in pieces that neither could achieve alone. This collaboration allows artists to push the boundaries of their imagination while leveraging the computational power of AI to execute their visions. It's a dance of creativity, where the artist directs, and the AI responds, creating harmony on the canvas.

Enhancing creative workflows is another realm where AI shines. Artists often feel bogged down by the mundane tasks of editing and refining their work. This is where AI steps in, offering tools that streamline these processes. Automated editing tools are a prime example, assisting with colour correction, image enhancement, and even video editing tasks. These tools free artists to devote more time to the conceptual phases of their projects, where their creativity truly shines. By handling repetitive tasks, AI allows artists to focus on what they do best: creating and innovating.

AI also acts as an extension of an artist's vision, bringing to life complex ideas that may have been difficult to achieve manually. Emotion recognition software exemplifies this by analyzing viewers' emotional responses to art, providing artists valuable feedback. This data can guide artists in crafting pieces that evoke specific emotions or tell more compelling stories. In doing so, AI not only aids in the creation of art but also its reception, enhancing the connection between the piece and its audience. This relationship transforms art into a dynamic conversation, where AI helps bridge the gap between intent and perception.

The world of fashion design offers a glimpse into how AI can revolutionize creative processes. Designers use AI to create innovative and adaptive fashion pieces that respond to environmental cues or consumer preferences. AI's ability to analyze trends and predict styles allows designers to stay ahead of the curve, crafting garments that are both stylish and functional. This collaboration between AI and fashion designers opens new possibilities for materials, patterns, and sustainability, pushing the industry toward a more dynamic future. AI's role here is not to replace the designer but to act as a muse, inspiring and facilitating their creative journey.

CASE STUDY: AI IN FASHION DESIGN

Consider the case of FINESSE, a fashion house that has fully integrated AI into its design and production process, replacing traditional designers with proprietary deep technology. Rather than relying on human intuition and trend speculation,

FINESSE's AI algorithms analyze vast datasets, including social media trends, past sales data, and consumer behaviour, to predict which styles will resonate with its audience. This data-driven approach eliminates the guesswork typically involved in fashion design and significantly reduces overproduction and waste by ensuring that only in-demand pieces are manufactured. By leveraging AI to streamline decision-making, FINESSE demonstrates how technology can drive creativity and sustainability in the fashion industry.

In the same way, AI, as a creative collaborator, offers artists in all fields new tools and perspectives. Whether automating workflows or enhancing emotional impact, AI supports artists in their pursuit of excellence. It invites them to explore uncharted territories of creativity, where human intuition and machine intelligence converge to create works of unparalleled depth and originality. This chapter serves as a testament to the power of collaboration, not just between artists but between artists and the technology that amplifies their potential.

1.3 DEMYSTIFYING AI FOR ARTISTS

Imagine the excitement of an artist as they first encounter AI— only to be met with a baffling mix of jargon that seems more suited to a computer science textbook than a creative studio. Terms like "machine learning" and "neural networks" can be as intimidating as a blank canvas to an artist. Let's simplify these concepts. Think of machine learning as teaching a computer to recognize patterns, similar to how you train a pet. Neural networks are the computer's brain, processing information and learning from it. Data sets are just collections of information AI uses to learn about the world, like an artist studying a portfolio of reference images. By breaking these terms down, let's remove the mystique surrounding AI, making it approachable for artists of all backgrounds.

Misunderstandings about AI abound, often fueled by Hollywood portrayals of machines with sinister motives. In reality, AI is not poised to replace artists anytime soon. Instead, AI excels at tasks involving pattern recognition and data analysis, leaving creativity's nuanced, emotive aspects firmly in human hands. For example, while AI can generate many art styles, it cannot replicate the personal experiences and emotions an artist infuses into their work. The myth that AI will dominate the art world is just that—a myth. By understanding what AI can and cannot do, artists can confidently embrace AI as a tool that complements their creativity.

For those new to AI, diving into this world can be daunting. Fortunately, there are platforms designed with beginners in mind. For instance, OpenAI's DALL-E and Ideogram offer accessible entry points for artists eager to explore AI. These tools simplify the process, allowing users to experiment with AI-generated art without needing a PhD in computer science. They provide intuitive interfaces that guide you through creating digital masterpieces with just a few clicks and prompts. By starting here, artists can gradually build their understanding and comfort with AI, paving the way for more advanced explorations.

Confidence in using AI grows with practice. Artists should start with simple projects that allow them to explore AI's capabilities without the pressure of creating a masterpiece. Consider experimenting with AI to generate abstract backgrounds or textures, enhancing your existing work with new dimensions. These trial projects offer a playground for creativity, encouraging artists to take risks and explore new possibilities. By engaging with AI in a low-stakes environment, artists can build the confidence to incorporate these tools into their regular workflow, ultimately enriching their creative practice.

1.4 OVERCOMING FEAR: MAINTAINING YOUR ARTISTIC IDENTITY

In art, the fear of losing one's unique style is akin to a chef losing their signature flavour. It's a concern that looms large, especially when AI enters the creative kitchen. Will the machine's algorithms dilute what makes your work distinct? Fear not, for AI can be a tool for amplifying rather than overshadowing your creative voice. Imagine it as a spice that enhances your dish, not overpowers it. You can maintain your style by thoughtfully blending AI outputs with traditional methods. Consider an artist who uses AI to generate complex patterns but applies them with a brush, merging digital precision with the warmth of human touch. This symbiosis ensures that AI serves your vision, not vice versa.

AI isn't here to replace your artistic identity; it's here to amplify it. Picture a musician using a custom AI filter that adapts their guitar's sound to echo their unique style. Similarly, artists can create personalized digital tools—filters and brushes that reflect their artistic signatures. These tools extend one's creativity, allowing the artist to explore new dimensions while staying true to their core style. These digital extensions don't just mimic your touch; they embody it, enabling you to produce work that is unmistakably yours yet enriched by AI's capabilities. This approach transforms AI from a potential threat into an ally that magnifies your creative expression.

Authenticity in art is paramount, and incorporating AI doesn't mean sacrificing it. In fact, AI can help preserve authenticity by embedding signature techniques within AI-aided projects. Artists can integrate their unique methods into AI workflows, ensuring the final output retains their personal touch. Imagine a sculptor who uses AI to simulate different lighting conditions for their work but carves each piece by hand, maintaining the integrity of their craft. This marriage of AI and personal technique produces innovative and authentic art, a testament to the artist's skill and vision in a modern context.

Success stories abound of artists who have maintained their identity while embracing AI. Take me, a photographer who's used AI to process thousands of images yet curate each selection with my own discerning eye. Or the digital artist who employs AI to generate intricate patterns and then incorporates these into larger works that bear their unmistakable style. These examples inspire, proving that AI can be a valuable collaborator in the creative process. They demonstrate that with careful integration, AI can enhance rather than compromise an artist's unique expression. My experiences and those of many others offer valuable insights into balancing AI integration with personal style, highlighting strategies to guide others on a similar path.

1.5 AI IN THE CREATIVE PROCESS: A BALANCED APPROACH

In the bustling hub of a modern design studio, an artist sits at a workstation flanked by both traditional tools and a sleek computer interface. The artist's task: to create a visual campaign for a new product launch. Here, AI doesn't just hover in the background; it actively participates. It suggests colour palettes, generates layout options, and even predicts trends based on current market data. This scenario exemplifies AI's true potential —not as a replacement for human creativity but as a valuable collaborator in the creative process. Understanding AI's capabilities and limitations is crucial to leveraging its power effectively. While AI excels at processing large datasets and generating patterns, it lacks the innate human ability to imbue art with emotion and narrative depth. Thus, AI is a powerful tool that amplifies human creativity rather than replaces it.

Integrating AI thoughtfully into existing artistic workflows requires strategic planning. Artists must evaluate how best to incorporate AI tools to complement their unique practices. For instance, a photographer might use AI to sort and enhance thousands of images swiftly, leaving more time for the nuanced process of curating a final collection. A painter might employ AI for preliminary sketches, providing a foundation to build with traditional techniques. These workflow integration plans allow artists to harness AI's strengths, optimizing efficiency without sacrificing personal touch. By strategically embedding AI into specific aspects of your work, you can unlock new dimensions of artistry, achieving a harmonious balance between technology and tradition.

Evaluating AI's role in personal projects necessitates critically assessing when and how to employ these tools. Artists should establish criteria for determining the suitability of AI in their endeavours, considering factors such as the project's complexity, desired outcomes, and personal comfort with technology. For example, a digital artist aiming to create a series of abstract designs might embrace AI for its ability to generate unpredictable patterns, while a sculptor focused on tactile experience might limit AI's involvement in the design phase. This evaluative process ensures that AI enhances rather than hinders creative expression. By critically assessing each project's needs, artists can make informed decisions about integrating AI, safeguarding the integrity of their vision.

Case studies across diverse artistic disciplines illustrate the successful balance of AI use. In graphic design, artists have utilized AI-driven software to streamline workflow and innovate with complex patterns. In music, composers have partnered with AI to generate harmonies and rhythms previously unimaginable, creating soundscapes that push the boundaries of auditory art. Even in traditional fields such as sculpture, AI has assisted artists in visualizing their creations in virtual spaces before making the first cut. These examples demonstrate AI's versatility and potential to complement various creative practices. By learning from these pioneering efforts, artists can confidently explore AI's possibilities, enriching their work and contributing to the evolution of art.

In the vibrant tapestry of today's creative landscape, AI emerges as a tool that, when used wisely, can enhance and elevate artistic endeavours. The key lies in understanding its capabilities and limitations, integrating it thoughtfully into workflows, and critically assessing its role in personal projects. By doing so, artists can maintain control over their creative processes while embracing the innovative potential of AI. Through balanced use, AI becomes a partner in the artistic journey, offering new perspectives and possibilities without overshadowing the unique voice and vision of the artist. As we continue to navigate the ever-evolving intersection of technology and creativity, the harmonious integration of AI stands as a testament to the enduring power of human ingenuity.

2 FOUNDATIONAL AI CONCEPTS FOR CREATIVES

Picture this: an artist sits in their studio, surrounded by various brushes, paints, and canvases. Yet, the most important tool isn't tangible. It's an algorithm humming quietly in the background, ready to assist in the creative process. This is the world of machine learning in art, where algorithms become your co-artist, ready to tackle creative challenges. Machine learning, at its core, involves teaching a computer to learn from data, much like how you might learn from observing a master painter at work. Machine learning opens doors to artistic possibilities once confined to dreams by analyzing patterns and making predictions based on vast amounts of information.

In machine learning, two primary methods are supervised and unsupervised. Imagine supervised learning as a guided art class where the teacher provides examples and feedback. Here, algorithms learn from labelled data, understanding the relationship between input and output. For instance, in creating digital artwork, supervised learning might involve feeding the algorithm thousands of images of landscapes to teach it the concept of a horizon. On the other hand, unsupervised learning is like an open studio session, where the algorithm explores data patterns without explicit guidance. This method can lead to unexpected and innovative results, such as discovering unique colour schemes or novel compositions that defy traditional norms. Together, these methods equip artists with tools to explore and push the boundaries of creativity.

The magic of machine learning lies in its ability to recognize patterns, a skill vital to any artist. By analyzing large datasets, these algorithms excel in identifying trends that might elude the human eye. Consider image editing, where machine learning can enhance photos by recognizing and adjusting for lighting inconsistencies. In music, algorithms identify rhythm and melody patterns, allowing composers to weave intricate compositions. This pattern recognition extends to various art forms, offering artists a new lens through which to view their work. By leveraging machine learning, you can uncover hidden structures and relationships in your creations, enriching your artistic expression.

Machine learning's applications in art are as diverse as they are exciting. Automated colour matching, for example, revolutionizes how artists approach colour theory and palette selection. By analyzing colour relationships in existing artworks, algorithms suggest harmonious schemes tailored to your creations. This tool becomes your digital colour consultant, offering insights that transform your understanding of hue and contrast. In writing, predictive algorithms assist in narrative development by suggesting plot twists or character arcs based on existing literary patterns. These applications empower artists to explore new dimensions of storytelling, where machine learning acts as a silent partner in crafting compelling narratives.

For those eager to dive into machine learning, beginner-friendly tools offer a gentle introduction. Google's Teachable Machine invites you to create simple AI models with minimal coding, perfect for experimenting with basic concepts. RunwayML, another accessible platform, provides a creative playground to explore machine learning's potential in art projects. These tools demystify the technology, making it approachable for artists of all backgrounds. By experimenting with these platforms, you gain hands-on experience that bridges the gap between curiosity and creation.

Reflection Section: Exploring Machine Learning in Your Art

Consider how machine learning might enhance your creative practice. Reflect on the following prompts:

1. How could supervised learning help refine your technique or style?

2. What unexpected results might unsupervised learning bring to your work?

3. In what ways could pattern recognition reveal new insights about your art?

Use these reflections to consider how machine learning might expand your creative horizons, offering new tools and perspectives on your artistic journey.

2.2 GENERATIVE ADVERSARIAL NETWORKS (GANS) EXPLAINED

Imagine a world where machines invent art, not accidentally or through mimicry, but through a structured dance of creation and critique. Enter Generative Adversarial Networks (GANs), the dynamic duo of AI that has shaken up the art world. At their core, GANs consist of two neural networks: the Generator, which creates new content, and the Discriminator, which evaluates it. Think of the Generator as an ambitious artist sketching out new ideas, while the Discriminator acts as the astute critic, identifying flaws and pushing for improvements. This iterative process of creation and evaluation allows GANs to produce content that is astonishingly realistic, blurring the lines between human and machine-generated art.

The relationship between the Generator and Discriminator is akin to a friendly rivalry. The Generator aims to create data indistinguishable from real-world examples, while the Discriminator works to spot the fake. Over time, this interaction refines both networks. As the Discriminator becomes better at identifying fake data, the Generator improves its ability to deceive. It's a bit like a game of cat and mouse, where each side continually ups its game. This dynamic interplay results in increasingly sophisticated outputs, allowing GANs to produce content that can surprise even the most discerning human eyes.

GANs have emerged as powerful tools for generating unique and striking pieces in innovative art creation. One notable application is the creation of AI-generated portraits. These portraits are crafted entirely from scratch, showcasing faces that have never existed in reality. The Generator synthesizes these images by learning from countless human faces, capturing subtle nuances that give each portrait a lifelike quality. Artists can then refine these portraits, adding their own touches to create a fusion of AI precision and human creativity. Beyond figurative art, GANs also excel in abstract art generation. By manipulating inputs and parameters, artists can explore new forms and compositions, often arriving at results that challenge traditional artistic boundaries.

However, working with GANs is not without its challenges. One significant hurdle is overfitting, where the Generator becomes too familiar with its training data, leading to outputs that lack originality. Bias is another concern, as GANs can inadvertently reproduce biases in their training datasets. These pitfalls require careful attention and mitigation strategies, such as diversifying training data and employing techniques to encourage creativity. By addressing these issues, artists can harness the full potential of GANs while safeguarding the integrity of their work.

The art world is already witnessing the impact of GANs through platforms like Artbreeder, which fosters collaborative generative artwork. Here, users can blend different images to create entirely new forms, allowing for a communal exploration of creativity. Another example is DeepArt, which utilizes GANs for style transfer. It enables artists to reimagine their images in the style of famous artworks or entirely new genres. These platforms high-light GANs' versatility, offering artists tools that expand their creative horizons and redefine the possibilities of digital art.

2.3 THE ROLE OF NEURAL NETWORKS IN CREATIVITY

Imagine your brain as a bustling metropolis of neurons, each firing off messages in a never-ending dialogue. Neural networks in computers attempt to mimic this complex system, albeit with less drama and more efficiency. They consist of layers of artificial neurons akin to tiny decision-makers, each connected by artificial synapses. These connections enable the network to learn from data and make informed predictions or decisions. Think of it as teaching a child to recognize a cat by showing them countless cat pictures until they can spot a feline in any form. This process allows neural networks to become adept at recognizing patterns, classifying objects, and even generating new content.

In image and sound processing, neural networks play a starring role. Their ability to enhance and restore images is nothing short of impressive. Consider an old, faded photograph brought back to life with vibrant colours and sharp details. Like a digital restoration artist, neural networks analyze the existing image and fill the gaps. These networks can remove noise, improve resolution, and even repair damaged sections, breathing new life into neglected visuals. In music, neural networks help create soundscapes that captivate and transport listeners. By analyzing existing sound patterns, they can synthesize new sounds, layering and modifying them to produce music that resonates with emotional depth.

The creative potential of neural networks extends beyond mere enhancement; they can learn and mimic artistic styles, offering artists new ways to experiment and innovate. For visual artists, this means the ability to emulate the styles of renowned painters or even invent entirely new ones. Imagine a digital brush that paints like Van Gogh but with your unique twist. By training on specific art styles, neural networks can apply these characteristics to new works, allowing for endless exploration of form and colour. This capability empowers artists to push the boundaries of their creativity, experimenting with styles that might have been technically challenging by hand.

Several tools harness the power of neural networks, making these advanced capabilities accessible to artists and designers. Take NeuralStyler, for instance, an application that transforms videos into artistic animations by applying different styles to each frame. It's like having a personal animation studio at your disposal, where every project can take on a life of its own, infused with artistic flair. These tools simplify complex processes and inspire artists to explore new dimensions of their work. They provide a playground where creativity meets technology, encouraging experimentation without fearing failure.

Neural networks, with their ability to simulate human-like learning, bring a unique blend of precision and creativity to the artistic process. As you experiment with these technologies, consider the endless possibilities they offer. From enhancing images to composing original music, the applications are as diverse as they are exciting. Embrace the opportunity to explore new creative territories, knowing that the digital brush is yours to wield.

2.4 STYLE TRANSFER TECHNIQUES FOR ARTISTS

Imagine blending the brushstrokes of Van Gogh with the vibrant hues of a modern-day photograph. This is the magic of style transfer, a process that allows you to take the stylistic elements of one image and apply them to another. It's like having a digital paintbrush that can transform your work with the flair of history's greatest artists. Style transfer, a fascinating application of deep learning, allows artists to reimagine their creations in extraordinary ways, challenging conventional art boundaries while enriching their visual vocabulary. By using algorithms to separate and recombine style and content, artists can effortlessly transform the mood and texture of their images. This technique has become a cornerstone in digital artistry, offering endless possibilities for innovation and exploration.

The style transfer process begins with image-to-image translation, a method where the algorithm identifies and isolates the stylistic features of a source image. Imagine a photograph of a serene lake. The photograph morphs into a vivid impressionist masterpiece by applying the fiery brushstrokes of a Van Gogh painting. This transformation isn't just a simple overlay; it's a nuanced blending that maintains the original structure while infusing it with new aesthetic qualities. As the algorithm learns the intricacies of the style, it reinterprets the target image, creating a fusion that's both familiar and new. This process opens up a world of possibilities for artists, allowing them to experiment with styles and techniques previously constrained by the physical medium.

Style transfer isn't confined to static images; its applications span various art forms, breathing new life into traditional disciplines. In photography, style transfer can elevate a mundane snapshot into a painterly piece, capturing the essence of classic artistry. Picture transforming a cityscape photo into a vibrant watercolour or an oil painting. The technique also finds a home in painting, where artists can reimagine their work in the style of different art movements, blending contemporary themes with historical aesthetics. Beyond static images, style transfer enhances visual styles in film and animation. Filmmakers can apply this technique to create seamless visual narratives, adding depth and texture to scenes in ways that evoke particular moods or artistic styles. Animation projects can incorporate this technique to bring unique stylistic flair to characters and backgrounds, creating a visually rich experience that captivates audiences.

For artists seeking to create personalized artistic styles, style transfer offers a dynamic toolset for developing unique visual signatures. You can craft a distinct aesthetic that reflects your creative vision by experimenting with different styles. Custom style creation involves training algorithms on your own artwork, enabling you to apply your artistic signature to new projects. Imagine having a digital brush that paints in your specific style, allowing you to maintain consistency across various pieces. This capability empowers artists to take ownership of their creative identity, blending technology with personal expression in a way that resonates with their audience. Custom styles distinguish your work and provide a platform for innovation, sparking new ideas and possibilities.

Several tools and software facilitate style transfer, making it accessible to artists of all experience levels. Apps like Prisma and DeepArt have gained popularity for their ease of use and stunning artistic results. With a few taps, your smartphone can transform any photo into a masterpiece, utilizing powerful algorithms to apply styles from iconic artworks or personalized designs. These apps provide an entry point for exploring style transfer, offering intuitive interfaces that simplify the process and inspire creativity. By experimenting with these tools, artists can explore various styles and techniques, expanding their creative repertoire and enhancing their visual storytelling.

2.5 AUGMENTED CREATIVITY: BEYOND THE DIGITAL CANVAS

Imagine stepping into an art gallery where the walls are alive, responding to your movements, and inviting you to interact with the exhibits. This is the realm of augmented creativity, where AI tools transcend traditional artistry and open up new avenues for creative expression. Interactive art installations are a testament to this evolution. They transform passive viewing into an immersive experience, captivating audiences and engaging them on a sensory level. Artists harness AI to create dynamic installations that adapt in real time, offering viewers a unique interaction every time they visit. These installations can respond to touch, sound, and even emotional cues, creating a symphony of human and machine harmony.

AI's influence extends into mixed media, blending digital and traditional elements to enhance creative expression. Picture a sculptor incorporating AI-driven projections that shift and change, enhancing the physical form with digital light and movement. This union between mediums invites artists to explore uncharted territories, breaking free from the constraints of a single discipline. Digital sculpting and painting tools enable creatives to experiment with forms and textures that would be difficult, if not impossible, to achieve by hand alone. These tools serve as a bridge, connecting the tactile world of physical art with the limitless possibilities of digital innovation.

Augmented Reality (AR) is another frontier in this expansive landscape, pivotal in creating dynamic and engaging art pieces. AR art exhibitions bring static works to life, overlaying digital content onto the physical world and offering audiences a layered experience. Imagine walking through a park where your phone or AR glasses reveal hidden digital sculptures hovering among the trees. These exhibitions push the boundaries of traditional art, creating spaces where reality and imagination intertwine seamlessly. They invite viewers to engage with art in a personal and interactive way, transforming public spaces into canvases of creativity.

Case studies in augmented creativity highlight the successful integration of AI and AR into the artistic process. One example is BrandXR's AR murals, which blend physical art with digital enhancements, allowing viewers to enter the artwork and interact with animated elements. Similarly, "The Journey" by Augmented Island Studios transforms a traditional mural into an immersive experience, enabling audiences to engage with augmented reality layers. Another innovative project, the "Warrior S3" Interactive AR Mural Experience, used AI and AR to transport users into a fully immersive world, adapting the artwork based on user interactions. These projects exemplify the collaborative potential of AI, where human imagination and technological prowess converge to create dynamic and personalized artistic experiences. Such endeavours demonstrate AI's power to expand artistic possibilities, challenging creators to rethink the boundaries of their craft and how audiences engage with art in the digital age.

As we conclude our exploration of foundational AI concepts for creatives, it's clear that the intersection of technology and art offers many opportunities for innovation. From enhancing traditional media to creating interactive experiences, AI empowers artists to push the limits of their creativity. This chapter has laid the groundwork for understanding how AI can augment the creative process, offering tools and techniques that are as varied as they are powerful. As we move forward, we'll delve deeper into the practical applications of these technologies, exploring how they can be integrated into your own artistic practice to create work that resonates with contemporary audiences.

3 PRACTICAL AI APPLICATIONS ACROSS CREATIVE FIELDS

I magine staring at a blank canvas, the digital cursor blinking expectantly, while your mind feels as empty as the white screen before you. For many artists, the initial spark of creativity can be the most daunting hurdle. Enter AI, your new brainstorming buddy, ready to jumpstart your creative process. AI tools are redefining artistic ideation, offering novel ways to generate and refine ideas. They serve as the muse you never knew you needed, helping you conjure up concepts you couldn't quite grasp on your own. These tools are not merely digital assistants but partners in your creative journey, ready to help you explore uncharted territories of imagination.

Regarding artistic ideation, AI tools like Artbreeder and Pinterest are invaluable. Artbreeder, for instance, allows you to morph and blend images to create new visual concepts, sparking ideas you might not have considered. It's like mixing paints in a digital palette, where each blend offers a new perspective. Meanwhile, Pinterest's AI-driven algorithms curate mood boards based on your preferences, pooling together an eclectic mix of inspirations across the web. It's like having a personal art curator who knows your tastes better than you do. These tools help you visualize your thoughts, turning abstract ideas into tangible project starting points. Using AI to fuel your creative brainstorming, you can jumpstart your projects with a fresh perspective and a wealth of ideas.

Once the ideas are flowing, AI plays a crucial role in creating art pieces. Programs like Adobe Fresco offer AI-enhanced brushes that simulate real-world painting techniques, providing a tactile experience in a digital environment. These brushes adapt to pressure and movement, allowing you to easily create intricate details and textures. It's as if the digital canvas has become an extension of your hand, responding fluidly to every stroke. This technology bridges the gap between traditional and digital art, offering the best of both worlds. By leveraging AI in digital painting, you can achieve the depth and richness of traditional media while enjoying the flexibility and convenience of digital tools.

AI-enhanced art techniques do not stop at creation; they extend into the realm of refinement and enhancement. One standout feature is AI-assisted colour correction, where tools like Adobe's generative AI adjust colour palettes to enhance the visual impact of your work. These tools analyze your piece and suggest adjustments that harmonize the colours, ensuring that every shade complements the overall composition. This saves time and ensures your work maintains a professional polish. By integrating AI into your artistic process, you can refine your creations precisely and easily, allowing you to focus on the creative aspects that matter most.

When it comes to exhibiting AI-generated art, innovation takes center stage. Virtual galleries and AI installations offer a dynamic way to present your work to a global audience. These platforms allow you to create interactive experiences where viewers can explore your art in immersive digital environments. Imagine an online gallery where visitors can wander through virtual rooms, each filled with your AI-enhanced creations, or an AI installation that responds to viewer interactions, creating a personalized experience for each visitor. These exhibitions not only showcase your work but also engage audiences in a unique and memorable way. AI transforms the traditional art exhibit into an interactive journey, captivating audiences and showcasing the potential of technology in the arts.

Reflection Section: Exploring AI in Your Art Practice

Consider how AI can transform your creative process. Reflect on these questions:

1. How might AI tools inspire new directions in your work?

2. What role could AI play in refining your artistic techniques?

3. How can virtual galleries expand the reach of your art?

Use these reflections to consider how AI might enhance your artistic practice, offering new opportunities for innovation and engagement with your audience.

3.2 ENHANCING MUSIC COMPOSITION WITH AI

Picture sitting in a dimly lit studio, headphones on, as the beat of a new song begins to form. You're a composer, and today, your collaborator is an algorithm. AI is reshaping how music is composed, making melody creation as seamless as brushing paint onto a canvas. Tools like Amper Music offer musicians a digital co-writer, crafting original melodies with the click of a button. You feed it your preferences—perhaps a chord progression or a genre—and it responds with an array of melodic suggestions. It's akin to having a musical brainstorming session, where ideas flow freely, and creativity is never constrained by writer's block. This process allows musicians to explore new harmonies and rhythms without the usual trial and error, unlocking potential that might otherwise remain untapped.

Beyond composing melodies, AI is making waves in music production and editing, transforming raw tracks into polished masterpieces. Platforms like LANDR automate mixing and mastering, tasks traditionally reserved for skilled engineers. With AI, you get a virtual sound engineer to analyze your track and make precise adjustments to balance levels and enhance clarity. It's like having an expert tweak every knob and dial, ensuring each note resonates perfectly. The process is efficient and accessible, enabling musicians to achieve professional-quality sound from the comfort of their home studios. AI's involvement in production doesn't just save time; it elevates the quality of music, allowing artists to focus on creativity rather than technical minutiae.

Collaboration with AI extends to creating entire compositions, where the AI serves as a virtual band member. Imagine working on a new track that needs a bass line or a drum sequence. AI steps in, generating instrumental tracks tailored to your style and specifications. These AI-generated segments blend seam-lessly with human elements, producing innovative compositions that push musical boundaries. Projects like these demonstrate AI's versatility, acting as both a tool and a partner in music creation. Musicians can experiment with genres and styles, knowing they have a reliable collaborator that adapts to their needs. This level of collaboration expands creative possibilities, enabling artists to explore sounds and ideas they might not have considered alone.

The impact of AI on music isn't confined to creation; it also revo-lutionizes how music reaches its audience. In the age of stream-ing, AI analyzes listener data, optimizing music distribution strategies. AI tools curate playlists based on user preferences, creating personalized listening experiences that cater to individual tastes. This data-driven approach ensures that each listener gets tailored tracks, enhancing engagement and discovery. For musicians, this means their music can reach the right audience more efficiently, increasing visibility and potentially boosting their careers. AI's role in music distribution exemplifies its power to connect creators with consumers, fostering a more dynamic and interactive music industry.

With AI at the helm, music composition and distribution are undergoing a transformation. Integrating AI into music allows for unprecedented levels of creativity and collaboration. Melodies are easily crafted, production is streamlined, and distribution is optimized. AI enriches music-making, offering musicians new tools and opportunities to express themselves. Whether you're an aspiring composer or an established artist, AI provides an ever-evolving landscape of possibilities to explore and conquer.

3.3 WRITING WITH AI: FROM PLOTTING TO PROSE

Picture a writer seated at their desk, staring at a blank page, the cursor blinking ominously. The task of weaving a narrative from thin air can feel daunting. Enter AI, a tool that transforms this blank slate into a playground of possibilities. AI applications in writing have evolved to become the writer's companion, assisting at every stage of the creative process. Let's start with story development, where AI tools like Plotagon step in. These automated plot generators act as co-writers, suggesting narrative structures and character arcs that might never have crossed your mind. You can watch the AI spin a web of potential plots by inputting basic story elements, each with twists and turns. It's like having endless story prompts at your fingertips, ready to ignite your imagination and guide you through the labyrinth of storytelling.

Refining your prose is another area where AI shines. Imagine having an editor who never sleeps, tirelessly refining your work for clarity and style. AI tools like Grammarly perform this role, offering suggestions to tighten your prose and eliminate grammatical errors. These tools enhance readability, ensuring your narrative flows smoothly from start to finish. In fact, I'm using it right now! It's like having a digital editor whispering in your ear, pointing out potential pitfalls and steering you toward polished perfection. With AI's assistance, you can focus on your creative vision, confident that writing mechanics are in good hands. Beyond grammar, AI can suggest stylistic changes, offering insights into how your writing can engage and resonate with readers more effectively.

Crafting dialogue and developing characters can be as challenging as it is rewarding. Here, AI offers a fresh perspective. AI character development tools provide detailed suggestions for character traits and backstories, helping you build complex, relatable personas. Imagine a character with a rich history and motivations that drive the plot forward—AI helps bring these characters to life by offering a foundation upon which you can build. Dialogue, too, benefits from AI's touch. These tools suggest realistic dialogue exchanges, ensuring your characters communicate authentically and compellingly. The result is a narrative that feels alive, with characters who leap off the page and draw readers into their world.

AI's influence extends beyond creation and into the realm of self-publishing and marketing. Once your manuscript is polished, AI-powered platforms will help you precisely target your book's audience. These tools analyze reader demographics and behaviours, ensuring your book lands in the hands of those who will appreciate it most. Imagine launching a marketing campaign that feels as tailored as a personal recommendation, each ad reaching the right eyes at the right time. AI's role in book marketing is transformative, allowing writers to connect with readers meaningfully. It's like having a marketing team at your disposal, one that understands the nuances of your work and knows exactly how to showcase it to the world.

In this new era of writing, AI is not replacing the writer but enhancing their craft. AI stands ready to assist from the initial spark of a plot idea to the final touches of a marketing campaign. Today's tools reshape how stories are told, offering writers new ways to engage with their craft and audience. As a writer, you hold the power to shape narratives that captivate and inspire, and with AI by your side, the possibilities are boundless.

3.4 AI IN GRAPHIC DESIGN: INNOVATION THROUGH AUTOMATION

In the bustling landscape of graphic design, AI has emerged as a formidable ally, streamlining processes that once consumed hours, if not days. Imagine sitting at your desk with a looming deadline, and in comes AI, your digital assistant, ready to take on the repetitive tasks that bog you down. One such innovation is AI-powered layout generators, which have transformed how designers approach projects. Tools like Canva have democratized design by automating layout creation. Whether crafting a sleek brochure or an eye-catching social media post, Canva's intuitive interface and AI-driven suggestions help you whip up professional designs in minutes. It's as if you have a team of seasoned designers whispering tips over your shoulder, ensuring your project shines. By automating these tedious tasks, AI frees you to focus on the creative aspects that truly matter, sparking innovation and elevating your work.

Beyond layouts, AI's prowess extends to crafting personalized design elements that align with unique brand identities. Custom logo generators, such as Looka, Wix Logo Maker, and Tailor Brands, stand at the forefront of this revolution, allowing businesses of all sizes to create logos that reflect their ethos. These tools analyze brand attributes, from colour schemes to industry trends, and generate logos that capture the brand's essence. It's like having a branding expert in your pocket, ready to distill your vision into a compelling visual identity. Platforms like Canva's Logo Maker and Brandmark further enhance customization, offering AI-powered suggestions that refine typography, layout, and design aesthetics. This technology empowers designers to produce tailored solutions that resonate with clients, enhancing brand recognition and loyalty. By leveraging AI's capabilities, you can create design elements that stand out in a crowded marketplace, setting your work apart with originality and flair.

AI doesn't just streamline; it also fuels creativity by encouraging designers to explore innovative approaches. AI-generated design variations offer a fresh perspective, presenting multiple options that inspire and challenge traditional norms. Imagine working on a project where you're stuck in a creative rut. An AI tool suggests alternative design paths, prompting you to consider angles you hadn't thought of. This feature catalyzes creativity, pushing the boundaries of what's possible and inviting experimentation. By presenting diverse design iterations, AI encourages you to explore unconventional solutions and push the envelope, resulting in groundbreaking work that captivates audiences and clients.

In the realm of user experience (UX) design, AI plays a pivotal role in enhancing interfaces and optimizing engagement. Predictive UX design tools like Hotjar and Google Optimize analyze user behaviour and preferences, providing insights that inform design decisions. These tools predict how users interact with a website or app, allowing designers to tailor elements for maximum impact. AI-powered design platforms like Adobe

Sensei and Figma's Magician plugin assist in automating repetitive tasks and generating intuitive UI elements, streamlining the creative process. Similarly, tools like Uizard can transform hand-drawn wireframes into functional prototypes, while Framer AI helps craft responsive layouts with intelligent suggestions. It's akin to having a crystal ball that reveals how users navigate your design, enabling you to craft intuitive and engaging experiences. By understanding user needs and preferences, AI helps create interfaces that are not only aesthetically pleasing but also functional and user-friendly. This results in designs that resonate with users, fostering positive interactions and driving success. The impact of AI in graphic design is profound, reshaping how we approach creativity and efficiency. AI is a cornerstone of modern design practices, from automating mundane tasks to sparking innovation. It empowers designers to focus on what they do best: creating compelling visuals that tell stories and connect with audiences. With AI by your side, the possibilities are endless, limited only by your imagination and willingness to explore new frontiers in design.

3.5 AI FOR INTERACTIVE MEDIA AND GAME DESIGN

In the realm of game development, AI has become an indispensable ally, shaping dynamic and immersive experiences that captivate players worldwide. One of the most exciting applications is procedural content generation (PCG), where AI crafts game content like levels, quests, and environments. Imagine a game where every time you play, the landscapes evolve, the challenges shift, and the quests surprise you anew. This is the magic of PCG, where algorithms work tirelessly behind the scenes to create fresh experiences.

A prime example of PCG in action is *No Man's Sky*, developed by Hello Games and released in 2016. Available on PlayStation,

Xbox, and PC, the game uses procedural algorithms to generate a vast universe containing over 18 quintillion planets, each with unique environments, weather conditions, gravity levels, and ecosystems. Every planet is formed based on algorithmic rules rather than manually designed, ensuring no two locations are identical.

Beyond just landscapes, *No Man's Sky* employs PCG for flora and fauna, resulting in distinct alien wildlife and plant life that vary in size, colour, and behaviour. The game also procedurally generates entire star systems, dictating planetary orbits, atmospheric compositions, and even the availability of resources. Additionally, alien species, their cultures, and languages are procedurally crafted, creating a sense of discovery as players learn to communicate with different civilizations scattered throughout the galaxy.

The game's ships, tools, and upgrades are also procedurally assembled, allowing players to discover and collect unique spacecraft with varying attributes. AI ensures that each new encounter, whether exploring an undiscovered world or interacting with NPCs, feels fresh and unpredictable. Developers use AI-driven procedural generation to create expansive game worlds and reduce development time, allowing them to focus on refining mechanics, storytelling, and player immersion.

By automating the creation of complex game elements, AI enhances gameplay, fosters player engagement, and enables developers to craft massive, living worlds that evolve dynamically. As *No Man's Sky* continues to receive updates expanding its procedural systems, it remains one of the most ambitious showcases of AI-driven game design in modern gaming.

AI's role doesn't stop at content creation; it extends into personalizing player interactions, making games feel uniquely tailored to each individual. Adaptive difficulty systems are a prime example of this personalization. These systems analyze player performance in real time, adjusting the game's difficulty to match skill levels. So, whether you're a novice or a seasoned pro, the game remains challenging but fair, providing just the right amount of tension to keep you invested. This dynamic adjustment ensures that players remain engaged without frustration, leading to longer play sessions and higher satisfaction. By adapting to player behaviour, AI creates a seamless experience where the game evolves alongside the player, providing a sense of growth and accomplishment.

In addition to adaptive difficulty, AI plays a crucial role in developing realistic character behaviour. Non-player characters (NPCs) are no longer mere background figures; they've evolved into lifelike beings with AI-driven logic. This allows NPCs to make decisions, react to player actions, and exhibit personalities. Imagine interacting with a shopkeeper in a virtual world who remembers your past interactions and adjusts their dialogue accordingly. This level of realism is achieved through AI algorithms that simulate human-like decision-making processes, lending depth and authenticity to game worlds. By enhancing NPC interactions, AI enriches the storytelling aspect of games, creating environments that feel alive and responsive.

Virtual and augmented reality (VR and AR) are other frontiers where AI significantly impacts interactive experiences. In VR environments, AI is used for real-time environmental adaptation, adjusting the virtual world based on user interactions. Picture a VR landscape that changes with your gaze, where AI modifies the scenery to maintain immersion and engagement. This adaptation extends to AR, where AI overlays digital content onto the real world, creating hybrid experiences that blend reality with imagination. Imagine an advanced version of *Pokémon GO*, experienced through AR glasses, where AI-driven creatures seamlessly integrate into your surroundings. As you walk through a city park, your AR glasses use AI to detect real-world objects—placing a Pokémon perched on a tree branch, hiding behind a bench, or even interacting with puddles and grassy fields. AI ensures that Pokémon react naturally to the environment, dodging obstacles, perching on ledges, or even scurrying under cars, making the experience feel lifelike.

AI could also introduce dynamic NPC trainers who appear in different locations and offer interactive challenges. These AI-driven characters could adjust their behaviour based on the player's level, location, or time of day, ensuring fresh and engaging encounters. Additionally, AR-integrated PokéStops and Gyms could evolve in real-time, offering different rewards or activities based on weather conditions, player density, or ongoing events. These applications highlight AI's ability to craft personalized, interactive experiences that push the boundaries of traditional media, transforming AR gaming into a deeply immersive, ever-evolving world that blurs the line between digital and physical reality.

Now, if you're wondering how to actually build something like this, well… that's a bit outside the scope of this book. (Unless, of course, you have an entire game studio at your disposal, in which case—why are you even reading this? Go make history!) But for the rest of us, Google is your best friend. There are plenty of AI-powered AR development tools out there, from Google ARCore to Niantic's Lightship ARDK, which help bring these kinds of experiences to life. Just be prepared for a long journey down the rabbit hole of documentation, coding, and inevitable existential crises when debugging AI behaviour.

To the point, AI's contribution to interactive media and game design is profound, offering tools and techniques that redefine how we engage with digital content. Through procedural content generation, adaptive difficulty, and realistic character behaviour, AI elevates gaming experiences to new heights. In VR and AR, AI's real-time adaptability transforms how we perceive and interact with virtual and augmented worlds, leading to richer, more immersive experiences. As we delve into the next chapter, we'll explore the ethical considerations and responsibilities of integrating AI into creative practices, ensuring that as we push the boundaries of innovation, we remain mindful of the impact on artists, audiences, and society at large.

4 ETHICAL CONSIDERATIONS IN AI ART

Picture this: you're walking through an art gallery and stop in front of a mesmerizing piece that seems to capture the essence of the cosmos. The colours swirl and dance in a way that feels both familiar and utterly alien. You lean in to read the plaque, expecting to find the name of a renowned artist, only to discover that the creator is... an algorithm. Welcome to the brave new world of AI art, where the lines between human and machine creativity blur, leaving us with a flurry of ethical questions and dilemmas as vibrant as the art itself. As an artist or creative, you stand at the crossroads of innovation and ethics, pondering this digital marvel's implications that challenge everything you thought you knew about art.

In the whirlwind of AI-generated art, the debate over authenticity versus automation takes center stage. On one hand, purists argue that art, in its truest form, is an extension of the human soul, a tangible reflection of personal experiences and emotions. On the other hand, AI enthusiasts see the machine's ability to produce art as a testament to human ingenuity, a new medium through which creativity can flourish. But where does that leave the art itself? Is it any less genuine because it was born from lines of code rather than brushstrokes? This conundrum raises essential questions about the nature of creativity and the value we place on human versus machine contributions. The National Art Education Association (NAEA) reflects on this, emphasizing the need to balance AI's potential with traditional art forms to ensure that individual expression doesn't become a casualty of technological progress.

The role of the artist in AI-assisted creations is another point of contention. When AI generates a piece of art, how much credit should the human artist receive? Are they mere facilitators, or do they play a more integral role in shaping the final product? It's a bit like baking a cake using a pre-made mix: you may not have milled the flour yourself, but your choice of ingredients and the way you decorate it make the cake uniquely yours. Similarly, artists working with AI must navigate the fine line between collaboration and authorship, ensuring their voice remains distinct amid the algorithmic cacophony. This dynamic invites a reevaluation of what it means to be an artist in the digital age, challenging creatives to redefine their roles in an ever-evolving landscape.

Ownership and attribution in AI art present a maze of legal and ethical challenges, akin to untangling a box of Christmas lights you swore you put away neatly last year. Who owns the rights to a piece of art created with AI assistance? Is it the artist, the software developer, or perhaps the AI itself? The U.S. Copyright Office, as noted in various sources, maintains that only works created by humans can be copyrighted, leaving AI-generated content in a legal gray area. However, the work may be eligible for copyright when human and AI collaboration leads to significant human contribution. This ambiguity opens the door to potential joint ownership models, where both humans and machines could share credit. Yet, even with these models, attribution challenges persist. Accurately crediting AI contributions can be as tricky as finding that elusive sock that always seems to vanish in the laundry.

Originality in AI-created works is a concept that demands careful consideration. In traditional art, originality is often measured by an artist's ability to present fresh perspectives and ideas. But when machines enter the fray, the definition of originality becomes murkier. Can AI truly create something new, or is it merely remixing existing concepts in novel ways? As artists grapple with these questions, they are forced to reevaluate long-held beliefs about creativity and artistic merit. AI's ability to analyze vast datasets and generate unique outputs challenges conventional notions of authorship, pushing artists to redefine what it means to be original in a digital age. The debate is reminiscent of the age-old question: if a tree falls in a forest and no one is around to hear it, does it make a sound? Similarly, if an AI creates art without human intervention, is it truly original?

The impact of AI on traditional artistic values cannot be overlooked. AI art challenges the very foundations of how we assess artistic merit, prompting a reevaluation of the criteria we use to judge art. In a world where machines can generate technically impressive works, the emphasis may shift toward the concept and intent behind the art rather than the execution itself. This shift encourages artists to focus on the stories they tell and the emotions they evoke rather than merely the techniques they employ. It also invites a broader discussion about the role of technology in shaping our cultural landscape as AI becomes an increasingly integral part of the creative process. As artists and creatives, you are tasked with navigating this complex and evolving terrain, finding ways to integrate AI's potential while preserving the essence of human expression.

Reflection Section: Ethical Considerations in
Your Creative Practice

As you explore the ethical landscape of AI art,
consider these questions:

1. How do you define authenticity in your work,
and how might AI challenge or enhance that
definition?

2. In collaborative projects with AI, how would
you navigate the balance between your role as
an artist and the contributions of the machine?

3. How can you ensure fair ownership and
attribution in your AI-assisted creations?

Reflect on these questions to inform your
approach to ethics in AI art and ensure that
your practice aligns with your values and
aspirations as a creative.

4.2 BALANCING INNOVATION AND RESPONSIBILITY

In the vibrant world of artistic innovation, maintaining ethical standards while pushing boundaries is like a tightrope walking in a swirling storm of colours and possibilities. It's thrilling, yet precarious. The role of ethics in artistic innovation cannot be overstated. Just as a painter must choose their palette wisely, artists working with AI must consider the ethical implications of their creations. Diving headfirst into the vast ocean of AI possibilities is tempting, but responsible experimentation is key. This means acknowledging the potential for bias, misinformation, and misuse that AI can bring. Artists must commit to understanding and actively mitigating these risks, ensuring their work contributes positively to society. Responsible AI experimentation involves a delicate balance of curiosity and caution, where artists embrace innovation without sacrificing their ethical compass.

Navigating the ethical use of AI tools requires more than just a basic understanding of their capabilities. It demands a conscientious approach that considers the impact of these tools on both the creative process and the wider world. Artists should familiarize themselves with ethical AI deployment guidelines, which offer best practices for using AI responsibly. These guidelines encourage transparency in AI use, advising artists to openly share how and why they integrate AI into their projects. This openness fosters trust, allowing audiences to appreciate the artistry while understanding the technology behind it. By adhering to ethical guidelines, artists create a foundation of integrity that supports their creative endeavours.

Maintaining artistic freedom while upholding ethical obligations presents a unique challenge. It's easy to feel constrained by rules and regulations, but these boundaries can inspire creativity. Think of them as the framework of a sculpture, providing structure while allowing for artistic expression. Artists can explore new forms and ideas within this framework, ensuring their work respects ethical guidelines without stifling their vision. Case studies of responsible innovation highlight artists who have successfully navigated this balance. These trailblazers demonstrate that pushing creative boundaries is possible while maintaining a commitment to ethical practices. Their work is a beacon for others, illustrating how ethics and innovation coexist harmoniously.

In collaborative AI projects, ethical concerns become even more pronounced. Ensuring that everyone upholds the same ethical standards is crucial when multiple parties work together. This involves creating collaborative ethical agreements that specify the responsibilities of each participant. Such agreements act as a roadmap, guiding the project and ensuring all parties understand their ethical obligations. They foster a culture of accountability, where each contributor is aware of their impact on the project and its ethical implications. By establishing clear guidelines, artists can confidently navigate the complexities of collaboration, knowing that their work aligns with their values.

As you explore the fascinating intersection of AI and art, remember that innovation and responsibility go hand in hand. By embracing ethical practices, you protect your work and contribute to a more thoughtful and inclusive artistic community. Each brushstroke, pixel, or note becomes part of a larger narrative that values integrity as much as creativity. This commitment to ethics is not a limitation but a lens through which you can view your work, ensuring it resonates with authenticity and purpose.

4.3 COPYRIGHT AND OWNERSHIP IN AI-GENERATED ART

Picture this: you've just created a stunning digital artwork with the help of an AI tool, and now you're ready to share it with the world. But before you hit "upload," a question lingers: who actually owns this masterpiece? AI-generated art presents a unique challenge in the realm of copyright and ownership, a landscape that's as complex as a Pollock painting. To navigate this terrain, it's crucial to understand the legal framework that governs copyright for AI-created works.

Current copyright laws, as they stand, are primarily designed for human creators. The U.S. Copyright Office, for instance, has made it clear that works created solely by AI, even when prompted by humans, lack copyright protection. It's like baking a cake without adding love or a personal touch—there's no personal authorship, thus no copyright. This stance raises significant questions for creatives using AI in their workflow. Can you claim ownership if the piece was largely generated by a machine? Where does the authorship line fall if you provide the initial concept and the AI does the heavy lifting? These are questions that the legal system is still grappling with, and as AI technology continues to evolve, so too will the legal interpretations and precedents surrounding creative works.

In Canada, copyright law, like in the U.S., is designed to protect works created by human authors. Under the Copyright Act of Canada, a work must originate from a human creator to qualify for copyright protection. The Canadian Intellectual Property Office (CIPO) has not explicitly addressed AI-generated works in depth, but legal interpretations suggest that purely AI-created content, without significant human intervention, is unlikely to receive copyright protection. It's akin to setting an autonomous machine loose in an art studio and calling yourself the artist—if the AI did all the heavy lifting, Canadian law is unlikely to recognize the human as the rightful copyright holder. However, if a human provides substantial creative input—such as curating, editing, or refining AI-generated material—it may still qualify for protection. As AI-assisted creativity becomes more prevalent, Canadian law must adapt to clarify the boundaries of authorship, ownership, and creative control in the age of machine-generated content.

The idea of AI as a co-creator further complicates matters. If you and an AI collaborate on a piece of art, does that make the AI an artist in its own right? While it sounds like a scenario from a sci-fi novel, it's a real-world dilemma. Legally, AI cannot be considered an author, as its outputs are based on algorithms and data sets. However, your role in guiding the AI, selecting styles, and making creative decisions can establish you as the rightful owner of the work. This is akin to working with an assistant who follows your instructions to bring your vision to life. The implications of AI as a co-creator are vast, potentially reshaping how we understand creativity and authorship in the digital age.

Establishing and protecting ownership rights for AI-generated art requires a savvy approach. It's essential to document your creative process meticulously, highlighting your contributions at each stage. This documentation shows your role in the creation, reinforcing your claim to authorship. When it comes to registering AI art with copyright offices, the process can be tricky. You must demonstrate significant human input and creativity, as the law favours human authorship. This might involve submitting a detailed account of your creative decisions, showing how you steered the AI towards achieving your artistic vision. While this process can be time-consuming, it's vital in safeguarding your rights and ensuring your creations are recognized and protected under existing copyright laws.

Legal precedents and landmark cases are beginning to shape the conversation around AI and copyright. Recent lawsuits, such as those filed by Getty Images against Stability AI, explore the boundaries of copyright infringement and highlight the complexities of using copyrighted materials in AI training. These cases underscore the importance of understanding and respecting intellectual property rights when working with AI. As more artists and organizations navigate these waters, the outcomes of these cases will likely influence future legislation, potentially leading to new guidelines for AI-generated content. These precedents serve as a reminder of the importance of staying informed and proactive in protecting your work, ensuring that your creative endeavours are both innovative and legally sound.

Understanding and navigating copyright and ownership is essential for any creative in the ever-evolving world of AI-generated art. By staying informed about current legislation, exploring the implications of AI as a co-creator, and establishing clear ownership rights, you can protect your work and continue to innovate confidently. As the legal landscape shifts, artists have the opportunity to shape the future of creativity, balancing the limitless possibilities of AI with the enduring value of human artistry.

4.4 ENSURING ETHICAL AI: GUIDELINES FOR CREATIVES

Imagine you're at the helm of a ship, navigating the vast ocean of AI creativity with a compass that points to innovation and integrity. This compass is your ethical framework—a set of guidelines that steer your creative projects towards responsible AI use. Developing such a framework is not about restricting creativity but ensuring that your work aligns with ethical principles that respect human and machine contributions. Start by considering ethical decision-making models, which serve as maps to guide your choices. These models help you weigh the potential impacts of your AI-driven art, balancing the scales between creativity and responsibility. By adopting these models, you create a structured approach to decision-making, ensuring that your artistic endeavours are groundbreaking and ethical.

Transparency and accountability are key pillars of ethical AI use. In a world where technology can sometimes obscure the origins of creativity, being clear about your use of AI is crucial. This means documenting your creative process meticulously, noting where and how AI tools have been employed. It's like leaving a trail of breadcrumbs, allowing others to trace your artistic journey from concept to completion. Disclosure practices involve openly communicating this information to your audience and providing insight into AI's role in your work. This transparency builds trust and invites viewers into the complex tapestry of human and machine collaboration, demystifying the process and reinforcing your credibility as an artist.

Fostering a culture of ethical creativity requires more than individual effort; it calls for a community-wide commitment to shared values. Artists, educators, and organizations must unite to promote ethical standards that guide AI use in the arts. Initiatives encouraging ethical AI practices provide a platform for this collective effort, creating a network of support and accountability. These initiatives can take many forms, from workshops and seminars to collaborative projects emphasizing ethical considerations. By participating in these efforts, you contribute to a culture that values creativity and ethics, ensuring that the art world remains a space where innovation thrives without compromising integrity.

Resources for ethical AI usage are like lighthouses, guiding you through the complexities of creative ethics. Organizations dedicated to AI ethics offer valuable guidelines and support, helping artists navigate the challenges of integrating technology into their work. These resources provide a wealth of information, from case studies and best practices to forums for discussion and collaboration. Engaging with these organizations enhances your understanding of ethical AI use and connects you with a broader community of creatives committed to responsible innovation. By tapping into these resources, you equip yourself with the tools and knowledge needed to create innovative and ethically sound art.

As we explore these guidelines, remember that ethical AI use is a dynamic process that evolves with technology and society. It challenges us to remain vigilant, thoughtful, and proactive in our creative practices, ensuring that our work reflects our values and aspirations as artists. With a strong ethical framework, you can confidently approach AI art, knowing that your creations contribute positively to the world. This chapter has highlighted the importance of ethics in AI art, offering a foundation for responsible creativity that respects human and machine contributions. As we move forward, we'll delve into the practical applications of these principles, exploring how they can enhance your artistic practice and enrich your creative journey.

5 STEP-BY-STEP GUIDES FOR AI INTEGRATION

Imagine standing at the edge of a vast, uncharted wilderness, equipped with nothing but a compass and a sense of adventure. This is what it feels like to step into the world of AI tools for the first time. As artists, designers, and creatives, you're about to embark on a journey to redefine your creative process, opening doors to new realms of possibility. But fear not! This chapter is your trusty guide, your map through the wilderness, leading you step by step into the enchanting world of AI art tools. Together, we'll explore selecting the right tools, setting up your creative space, and experimenting with AI to elevate your art. Whether you're a seasoned artist seeking new inspiration or a beginner eager to dive into digital creativity, this is your gateway to understanding and integrating AI seamlessly into your workflow.

5.2 Getting Started with AI Tools in Art

Selecting the right AI tools is like choosing the perfect brush for a painting or the ideal camera for a photoshoot. It's about finding the right match for your artistic goals and style. Begin by considering the criteria for tool selection. Ease of use is paramount, especially for those just dipping their toes into the AI waters.

Look for intuitive interfaces that don't require a degree in computer science to navigate. Cost is another factor; while some AI tools come with hefty price tags, others, like Stable Diffusion and Leonardo AI, offer free or affordable options that deliver impressive results. Compatibility with your existing workflow is crucial. Ensure your chosen tools seamlessly integrate with your existing software, like Adobe Creative Cloud. This integration will make the transition smoother and less disruptive to your creative process.

Popular AI art tools like DeepArt and RunwayML have become staples in the creative community. DeepArt allows you to transform photos into paintings by applying artistic styles, making it perfect for those looking to add a touch of classical elegance to their work. RunwayML, on the other hand, is a powerhouse for multimedia projects, offering a suite of tools that enable AI-assisted image and video editing. Both platforms provide user-friendly interfaces and tutorials to help you get started, making them excellent choices for artists new to AI. As you explore these tools, consider how they align with your creative vision and what unique capabilities they offer that can enhance your work. By taking the time to research and experiment with different options, you'll find the tools that best support your artistic endeavours.

Setting up your AI workspace is like preparing a stage for a performance. It requires thoughtful planning and the right equipment to ensure everything runs smoothly. Start with the hardware requirements. A computer with a robust graphics card and ample RAM (16 Gigabytes or more... Preferably, more) will handle the demands of AI processing. While you don't need a supercomputer, a mid-range device with these specifications will serve you well. As for software, ensure your operating system is up-to-date and compatible with the AI tools you plan to use. Installing the necessary software, such as Python, for certain AI programs may also be required. With your hardware and software in place, you can create an environment that fosters creativity and experimentation, allowing AI to become a natural extension of your artistic practice.

Understanding the basic functionality and features of popular AI tools is akin to learning the chords of a new song. It sets the foundation for creativity to flourish. Many AI tools offer image processing capabilities that enhance your art in ways traditional methods can't. For instance, AI-driven filters can adjust lighting, colours, and textures precisely and quickly, transforming ordinary images into extraordinary works. These features enable you to experiment with styles and effects easily, allowing you to explore new creative directions without fearing irreversible mistakes. By familiarizing yourself with these capabilities, you can unlock the full potential of AI tools, using them to enhance your work and push the boundaries of your artistic expression.

Experimenting with AI tools is where the real magic happens, much like mixing colours on a palette to discover new shades. Start with small projects to build familiarity and confidence. For example, AI can be used to enhance a simple photograph, applying different filters and styles to see how they alter the image. This exercise will help you understand the tools' functionalities and how they can be integrated into your workflow. As you become more comfortable, challenge yourself with more complex projects, such as creating a series of AI-enhanced artworks or experimenting with video editing. These starter projects are not only a great way to learn but also an opportunity to discover new creative possibilities. By embracing experimentation, you open yourself to a world of innovation, where AI becomes a valuable partner in your artistic journey.

Reflection Section: Your AI Art Toolkit

Consider creating a checklist of AI tools and
features that align with your creative goals.
Include ease of use, cost, compatibility, and
unique capabilities. Reflect on how each tool
can enhance your art and what new
possibilities it opens up.

This exercise will help you make informed
decisions and build a personalized AI toolkit
that supports your artistic vision.

5.3 IMPLEMENTING AI IN YOUR DESIGN WORKFLOW

Imagine you're at your desk, a blank screen before you, and a
deadline approaching. It's time to bring AI into the mix to transform your design workflow from a tangled mess of ideas into a
streamlined symphony of creativity. Integrating AI into your
design processes can feel like adding a new instrument to your
orchestra. With AI, you can enhance every stage of your design
work, from the initial spark of inspiration to the final polished
product. AI tools can act as a brainstorming partner for ideation
and concept development, offering a fresh perspective you
might not have considered. They help you visualize concepts by
generating mood boards, colour palettes, and even full-fledged
design mockups based on your input. These tools analyze
existing trends, offering insights that inspire new directions.
Imagine having access to a virtual think-tank that provides
endless visual prompts, fueling your creativity and helping you
overcome the dreaded creative block.

Designers often find themselves bogged down by repetitive
tasks that can sap the creative energy right out of them. This is
where AI shines brightly, automating mundane tasks like
resizing images or adjusting layouts. Think of AI as your digital

assistant, tirelessly managing these tasks so you can focus on the creative aspects that truly matter. Tools like Adobe Illustrator's Generative Recolor or Photoshop's Generative Fill automatically apply styles and adjustments, freeing up time for innovation. The result? A workflow that's as efficient as it is creative, allowing you to experiment freely without the burden of manual labour.

AI enhances creativity not by replacing it, but by augmenting it. Various tools exist that offer design variations and suggestions based on user preferences, helping creatives explore new directions and refine their work. Adobe Firefly and DALL·E allow designers to generate images from text prompts, providing instant visual inspiration and rapid prototyping. Platforms like the aforementioned RunwayML and Figma's AI-powered plugins (such as Magician) assist in real-time design editing, offering alternative approaches to creative challenges. Canva Magic Design suggests layouts, colours, and styles, streamlining the process for those looking to iterate quickly. Meanwhile, Autodesk Dreamcatcher generates structural design solutions based on user constraints, pushing the boundaries of product and industrial design. Even something as fundamental as colour selection is enhanced with AI tools like Khroma, which learns a designer's preferences and generates custom palettes. It's like having a seasoned design mentor offering guidance and insights, helping you push the boundaries of what's possible. This process inspires new ideas and streamlines creative exploration, enabling you to iterate quickly and efficiently. With AI in your corner, you can take risks and try out-of-the-box ideas, confident that you have a safety net of support and suggestions.

Collaboration and feedback within design teams are crucial to the evolution of any project, and AI is transforming these aspects too. Figma integrates AI to enhance team workflows, enabling real-time collaboration and feedback. Imagine the entire team working on a design project simultaneously, making adjustments and sharing ideas in real-time. AI facilitates this seamless inter-action, suggesting changes and improvements as you go. This dynamic environment fosters creativity and innovation, allowing for a fluid exchange of ideas and ensuring everyone is on the same page. By integrating AI into your collaborative processes, you create a workspace that thrives on synergy and collective creativity.

Let's look at real-world examples of how AI is used in design studios worldwide. Consider a design project where AI signifi-cantly impacted the process: a branding agency tasked with creating a new visual identity for a tech startup. The team employed AI to generate initial design concepts, analyze market trends, and automate tedious tasks like resizing and formatting. The result was a cohesive brand identity that resonated with the target audience and stood out in a crowded market. By lever-aging AI, the team delivered a polished product faster and more efficiently than ever before, demonstrating the transformative power of AI in the design world.

5.4 AI-POWERED ANIMATION: BRINGING IDEAS TO LIFE

Imagine bringing your animated characters to life with the flick of a digital wand. This is the power of AI in animation, where technology simplifies and enhances every step of the process, transforming your creative visions into dynamic realities. Tools like Adobe Character Animator are changing the game using AI to streamline animation. This software allows you to animate characters by capturing your facial expressions and movements, syncing them with your digital creation in real time. It's like having a virtual puppet show at your fingertips. You act, and your character mimics you instantly, reducing the time-consuming frame-by-frame animation to almost nothing. With features like automatic lip-syncing and motion capture, Adobe

Character Animator makes it possible to produce professional-quality animations with ease, giving you more time to focus on storytelling and character development.

In the pre-production phase, AI is your strategic partner, aiding in planning and organizing animation projects. Storyboarding, once a meticulous and laborious task, is now revolutionized by AI-assisted tools. Software like Storyboard Pro provides a dynamic canvas where you can sketch out your narrative flow, organizing scenes with precision. AI assists by suggesting camera angles, transitions, and even dialogue pacing, ensuring that your storyboard is not only detailed but also engaging. These tools allow you to experiment with different narrative structures, providing a clear roadmap for your animation project. Imagine the confidence you gain when every scene is mapped out and every plot twist is visualized before you even begin animating. This strategic planning sets the foundation for a smooth production process, where creativity is guided by clarity.

As you progress to generating animation assets, AI steps in as a creative assistant, offering tools that create characters, backgrounds, and more. AI-generated character models are a blessing for animators, providing lifelike figures that can be customized to suit any narrative. Whether you're crafting a whimsical fairy tale or a gritty sci-fi epic, AI helps generate characters with realistic movements and expressions, adding depth and authenticity to your story. Tools like Blender and Daz 3D offer libraries of characters and assets that can be adapted to fit your unique style. These AI-generated models are not just placeholders; they're dynamic elements that breathe life into your animation, allowing you to focus on refining the narrative and visual storytelling.

When it comes to post-production, AI continues to play a crucial role in polishing animated content. Colour grading and special effects, once the domain of specialized artists, are now accessible to all, thanks to AI. Tools like DaVinci Resolve use AI to apply professional-grade colour corrections, enhancing the visual quality of your animation. The software analyzes each frame, ensuring consistent colour balance and saturation, making your work visually cohesive. It also offers AI-driven effects that add flair and depth, from dynamic lighting adjustments to intricate particle effects. These enhancements elevate your animation, transforming it from a simple sequence of images into a captivating visual experience. With AI handling the technical details, you can concentrate on refining the emotive elements of your story, crafting a narrative that resonates with your audience.

Integrating AI in animation is not just about efficiency; it's about expanding your creative horizons. By simplifying complex processes and offering advanced features, AI empowers you to explore new ideas and push the boundaries of your craft. Whether you're an aspiring animator or a seasoned professional, AI provides the tools and support needed to bring your animated visions to life, transforming your imagination into reality with unprecedented ease and precision.

5.5 CRAFTING ORIGINAL SOUNDSCAPES WITH AI

Picture yourself as a composer in a bustling digital studio, surrounded not by traditional instruments but by a symphony of algorithms and software that promise to bring your musical ideas to life. This is the world of AI-driven music composition, where platforms like AIVA, Soundraw, and Boomy offer the tools to craft original soundscapes with ease. AIVA serves as your virtual partner, capable of generating unique compositions in various styles, from classical symphonies to cinematic scores. Soundraw enables dynamic, AI-assisted music generation, allowing users to tweak compositions in real time. Boomy, on the other hand, focuses on user-friendly, automatic track creation, making it easy for anyone to generate and even publish AI-generated music. It's like having an orchestra at your fingertips, ready to explore any genre or mood you desire. You simply provide the parameters—be it tempo, key, or style—and watch as the AI creates a musical tapestry tailored to your vision. The possibilities are endless, and the results can be as surprising as they are inspiring, offering new avenues for creativity and exploration.

Once you've composed a piece, integrating AI into the sound design process becomes a seamless next step. AI excels in sound layering and mixing, which assists in creating complex auditory landscapes that captivate listeners. Imagine building a multi-layered track, where each sound is meticulously placed to create a rich and immersive experience. AI tools analyze these layers, optimizing the balance and cohesion of the mix. They adjust levels, enhance frequencies, and ensure that each element complements the others, resulting in a polished and professional sound. This technology, much like a seasoned sound engineer, allows you to focus on the artistic aspects of your work, confident that the technical details are in expert hands.

Customization is key when working with AI-generated sounds. These digital compositions can be tailored to fit your specific creative vision, ensuring they resonate with your artistic intent. Editing and modifying AI outputs is akin to sculpting a block of marble into a masterpiece. You start with a foundation provided by the AI, then refine and shape the music to align with your goals. This may involve tweaking individual notes, altering tempo, or adding effects to enhance the emotional impact. By personalizing these sounds, you infuse them with your unique style, transforming them from generic compositions into bespoke creations that reflect your identity as an artist.

AI's impact on professional soundscapes is already evident in the world of film and gaming. Consider the intricate soundtracks of modern films, where AI has been utilized to create compelling scores that enhance narrative and emotion. It provides composers the tools to experiment with unconventional sounds and structures, crafting scores that push the boundaries of traditional music. In gaming, AI-generated music adapts in real-time, responding to player actions and creating a dynamic auditory experience. This adaptive music immerses players in the game world, making each play unique and engaging. Projects like these demonstrate how AI can elevate sound design, making it an integral part of storytelling and interactive media.

The use of AI in crafting soundscapes is as much about innovation as it is about artistry. It provides a platform for you to experiment with new ideas, transforming abstract concepts into tangible auditory experiences. Whether you're composing a film score, designing sound for a game, or simply exploring new musical directions, AI offers the tools and support to bring your creative visions to life. With AI's assistance, you can craft soundscapes that are not only original but also deeply resonant, capturing the essence of your artistic voice.

5.6 AI FOR CONTENT CREATION: WRITING SMARTER, NOT HARDER

Picture yourself at a cluttered desk, drowning in drafts and notes, with a looming deadline and a blank screen taunting you. Enter AI-powered writing assistants, your new best friends in the quest for clear, compelling prose. These digital companions, like Grammarly and Hemingway, revolutionize how we approach writing and editing. They don't just correct typos; they elevate your writing by suggesting nuanced improvements, enhancing clarity, and ensuring your voice remains strong. Grammarly, for instance, goes beyond grammar checks, offering style advice and tone adjustments. Hemingway, on the other hand, simplifies complex sentences, ensuring your message is as sharp as your wit. These tools act as editors in your pocket, helping you refine your work precisely and easily, so you can focus on the creative aspects that truly matter.

Yet, AI's role in content creation extends far beyond editing. It streamlines the entire process, from structuring ideas to crafting coherent narratives. Imagine having a digital architect for your thoughts, organizing them into a logical, compelling outline. AI tools excel at this, analyzing your notes and suggesting structures that enhance flow and coherence. They help you map out your work, ensuring each section builds on the last. This organization is invaluable, especially when tackling complex topics or lengthy projects. With AI's assistance, daunting writing tasks become manageable, allowing you to approach your work with confidence and clarity. By providing a framework for your ideas, AI frees you to focus on developing rich, engaging content that captivates your audience.

But AI isn't just about making writing easier; it's about making it more creative. AI-generated suggestions offer fresh perspectives, sparking new ideas and styles. These tools serve as digital muses, providing prompts that inspire creativity. Whether you're stuck in a narrative rut or exploring new genres, AI can suggest themes, plot twists, or character arcs that breathe new life into your work. Imagine having an endless supply of creative stimuli, each prompt a potential masterpiece waiting to be written. This capability challenges you to explore uncharted territories in your writing, experimenting with styles and ideas that push your creative boundaries. By embracing AI's suggestions, you open yourself to a world of possibilities where innovation and artistry combine to produce work that's both original and impactful.

Real-world examples highlight AI's transformative impact on publishing and content marketing. Consider a digital magazine that uses AI to tailor content for its diverse readership. By analyzing reader preferences, AI tools optimize articles to resonate with specific audiences, ensuring each piece is relevant and engaging. These AI-driven marketing campaigns don't just increase readership; they deepen engagement, fostering a loyal community of readers. By leveraging AI's analytical power, content creators can craft targeted messages that speak directly to their audience's interests and needs. This personalization enhances the reader's experience, transforming casual visitors into devoted followers. Through AI, content becomes more than words on a page; it becomes a dialogue, a connection between creator and consumer that enriches both.

As we explore these applications, it's clear that AI is not merely a tool for efficiency but a catalyst for creativity and connection. It offers writers the support and inspiration needed to craft compelling narratives that resonate with readers. By integrating AI into your content creation process, you gain a powerful ally that enhances your work, whether you're penning the next great novel or crafting an engaging blog post. With AI's help, you can write smarter, not harder, producing content that captivates, engages, and inspires.

MAKE A DIFFERENCE WITH YOUR REVIEW

UNLOCK THE POWER OF CREATIVITY

"Creativity is contagious. Pass it on." — Albert Einstein

When we share what we know and love, we help others grow. Let's spark that creative magic together!

Would you help someone just like you—curious about AI and creativity but unsure where to start?

My mission is to make AI tools simple, fun, and accessible for every creative mind. But to reach more artists, designers, and dreamers, I need your help.

Most people choose books based on reviews. So, I'm asking you to help a fellow creative by leaving a review.

It costs nothing and takes less than a minute, but your review could inspire someone to:

...dare to try a new art form. ...turn a creative hobby into a career. ...streamline their work and unlock new ideas. ...discover the confidence to experiment fearlessly ...take the first step toward their big dream.

To make a difference, simply scan the QR code below and leave a review:

[https://www.amazon.com/review/review-your-purchases/?asin=BOOKASIN]

If you love helping others create and grow, you're my kind of person. Thank you from the bottom of my heart!

— Arden Vale

6 INSPIRING CASE STUDIES AND SUCCESS STORIES

Picture yourself standing in a bustling art gallery, surrounded by a sea of curious onlookers, each captivated by a peculiar digital portrait that seems to gaze back at them. This isn't your typical art exhibition. The portrait is the brainchild of a machine, crafted with the guidance of an artist who sees algorithms not as cold, calculating entities but as creative companions. Welcome to the world of AI art pioneers, who are not only redefining what it means to create but are also challenging the very boundaries of artistic expression.

Take Mario Klingemann, a trailblazer in the AI art community renowned for his innovative use of Generative Adversarial Networks (GANs). Klingemann's work delves into the depths of human likeness, producing digital portraits that evoke intrigue and introspection. His piece "Memories of Passersby I" exemplifies this, where neural networks continuously generate portraits in real-time, each face unique and fleeting. Klingemann likens AI to a complex instrument, akin to a piano, where human agency and intuition guide the creation process. He navigates the challenges of working with neural networks, emphasizing trial and error to maintain a distinct creative voice. Through his art,

Klingemann explores themes of identity and authorship, inviting viewers to question the nature of creativity itself.

Meanwhile, Sougwen Chung takes a different approach, choosing to collaborate with AI in a more tangible form. Her robotic partners, affectionately named Doug (Drawing Operations Unit, Generation Four), join her in creating dynamic, hybrid artworks that blend human intuition with mechanical precision. These robots, which Chung designed and built herself, respond to her brain-wave data, creating a seamless feedback loop between artist and machine. Chung's performances, often streamed to global audiences, showcase this partnership, challenging traditional narratives of competition between humans and AI. Instead, she promotes collaboration, using AI to capture and translate human motion into expressive art. Her work invites us to rethink our relationship with technology, emphasizing harmony over hierarchy.

Both Klingemann and Chung employ unique methodologies in their artistic endeavours. For these artists, AI acts as a muse, sparking unconventional ideas and pushing the boundaries of traditional art forms. The process involves algorithmic experimentation, where artists iterate with AI to achieve outcomes that are as surprising as they are profound. This iterative dance between human and machine allows artists to explore new dimensions of creativity, where the unexpected becomes the norm and innovation thrives. It's a reminder that the creative process is as much about discovery as it is about execution, and AI provides a fertile ground for both.

The impact of these pioneering artists extends far beyond their own work, influencing perceptions and practices within the broader art community. Their art has graced prestigious exhibitions, earning accolades that celebrate the fusion of technology and creativity. Klingemann's work, for instance, has been recognized at events like Ars Electronica, while Chung's installations have captivated audiences at venues worldwide. These exhibitions not only showcase the potential of AI in art but also promote dialogue about its role in shaping the future of creativity. By challenging traditional boundaries, these artists inspire others to explore the possibilities of AI, encouraging a shift in how we perceive and engage with art.

For aspiring AI artists, the journeys of Klingemann and Chung offer valuable lessons. Embrace risk and innovation, they urge, for it is within the realm of the unknown that creativity flourishes. AI should not be used as a tool to replicate the familiar but as a catalyst for exploring uncharted territories. By taking creative risks, you open yourself to new perspectives and experiences, allowing art to evolve in unexpected and transformative ways. Remember that while AI can offer new avenues for expression, your unique vision remains the guiding force. Let AI be your partner, your muse, and together, you can redefine the boundaries of what's possible in the art world.

6.2 AI IN FILM: ENHANCING VISUAL STORYTELLING

Imagine sitting in a theatre, popcorn in hand, as the opening scene of a film unfolds with a breathtaking landscape that seems to stretch beyond the screen's edges. This immersive experience, capturing the realism of a world crafted from pixels, is a testament to the transformative power of AI in filmmaking. Filmmakers today are leveraging AI to weave more compelling narratives and craft dialogue that resonates with audiences, breathing new life into the ancient art of storytelling. AI assists in scriptwriting by analyzing plot structures and character arcs, paving the way for engaging and innovative stories. Projects like those utilizing Natural Language Processing (NLP) demonstrate how AI can suggest plot twists and character interactions, refining narratives in ways that captivate even the most discerning viewer. It's as if AI has become an unseen collaborator, working silently but powerfully to enhance the storytelling process.

Beyond the script, AI technologies are revolutionizing the nuts and bolts of film production. Virtual cinematography, for example, uses AI to create hyperrealistic environments and scenes that transport audiences to new worlds without ever leaving their seats. This technology allows filmmakers to design entire landscapes with a level of detail and authenticity that was once unimaginable. Imagine crafting a bustling cityscape or a serene alien planet, all from the comfort of a studio. The precision of AI-driven virtual cinematography enables filmmakers to experiment with lighting, angles, and perspectives, offering a playground for creativity unbounded by the limitations of physical sets. The result is a cinematic experience that is as visually stunning as it is immersive, drawing viewers into a seamless blend of reality and imagination.

The editing room, often the heart of film production, has also felt AI's transformative touch. Automated editing tools streamline the post-production process, allowing editors to focus more on creative decisions rather than technical details. AI systems can sort through hours of footage, identify key scenes, and even suggest edits, making the process efficient and innovative. This saves time and opens up new avenues for creativity, as filmmakers can experiment with various cuts and sequences without the laborious manual work. It's like having a digital assistant who never tires, always ready to offer a fresh perspective or a quicker path to the perfect scene.

AI's influence is equally profound in the realm of special effects, where it enables the creation of visuals that defy the boundaries of reality. Deepfake technology, despite its controversies, has become an essential tool for enhancing character portrayal. By seamlessly blending actors' faces with digital creations, deepfakes allow for performances that are as believable as they are revolutionary. Imagine a historical drama where an actor embodies a long-gone figure with uncanny accuracy or a sci-fi epic where characters transform before our eyes. However, this technology raises ethical concerns as the line between fiction and reality blurs. Filmmakers must navigate these waters carefully, ensuring deepfakes enhance the narrative without deceiving the audience.

The relationship between films and their audiences is evolving, with AI playing a crucial role in tailoring content to viewer preferences. Predictive audience analytics use AI to sift through mountains of data, identifying trends and preferences that shape how films are marketed and presented. This data-driven approach ensures that films resonate with their intended audiences, maximizing engagement and satisfaction. It's like having a crystal ball that reveals what viewers want before they know it themselves. By understanding audience behaviour and preferences, filmmakers can craft experiences that are both personal and universal, ensuring that their stories find the right audience at the right time.

In the dynamic world of film, AI is proving to be a catalyst for change, offering tools and techniques that push the boundaries of what's possible. From scriptwriting to special effects, AI enriches the filmmaking process, enabling creators to tell stories in ways that are more engaging, innovative, and visually stunning than ever before. As filmmakers continue to explore the potential of AI, the future of cinema looks brighter and more imaginative, promising experiences that will captivate audiences for years to come.

6.3 INTERACTIVE INSTALLATIONS: AI MEETS ART

In the hushed halls of a modern museum, the typical visitor might expect the usual quiet contemplation of art. But today, a new kind of exhibit beckons—a space where art and technology converge to create an immersive symphony of sights and sounds. These AI-driven interactive artworks do more than hang on walls; they engage, respond, and transform with each visitor's presence. Imagine installations where AI systems detect movement and adjust the ambiance accordingly, altering lighting and soundscapes to reflect the ebb and flow of human interaction. This seamless integration of AI into art spaces offers a dynamic experience where each visitor's journey through the gallery is unique, guided by the subtle responses of the surrounding technology.

Take "The Next Rembrandt" project, a striking example of AI's potential to breathe new life into the art world. By meticulously analyzing the works of the Dutch master, AI crafted a new painting in Rembrandt's style, capturing the essence of his technique while introducing a modern twist. This project was more than an exercise in replication; it was a dialogue between the past and present, inviting audiences to explore the intersection of historical artistry and contemporary technology. Visitors to the exhibition were not merely observers but participants in a broader conversation about creativity and the evolving role of AI in art. The painting, a testament to AI's ability to emulate artistic genius, sparked discussions about authenticity, originality, and the future of creative expression.

AI technologies are reshaping how art is displayed and experienced in physical spaces. Imagine entering a gallery where the environment subtly shifts in response to your presence. The lighting dims as you approach a piece, drawing you into its narrative, while ambient sounds adjust to complement the mood. Such responsive environments are made possible by AI, which processes sensor data and adapts the installation in real time. This technology creates a personalized experience where art becomes an interactive dialogue between the viewer and the exhibit. The boundaries of traditional art spaces are expanded as static displays transform into living, breathing entities that react to the nuances of human interaction. In these spaces, AI serves as a bridge between the tangible and intangible, crafting experiences that resonate on a deeply personal level.

The impact of AI installations on audience perception and engagement is profound. By offering real-time feedback and adaptation, these installations invite viewers to explore art in new and meaningful ways. Rather than passively observing, visitors are encouraged to engage, interact, and reflect, deepening their connection to the work. Imagine an exhibit where your movements influence the artwork's evolution, creating a dynamic interplay that blurs the line between creator and observer. This level of engagement fosters a sense of ownership and participation, transforming how audiences perceive and interact with art. The result is an enriched experience where art becomes a collaborative endeavour shared between the artists, technology, and the audience.

As AI continues to integrate into art spaces, the innovation potential is limitless. Artists and technologists are exploring new ways to harness AI's capabilities, creating installations that challenge conventional notions of art and audience. These interactive exhibits not only captivate and inspire but also provoke thought and conversation, inviting us to reconsider the role of technology in shaping our cultural landscape. Through AI, art becomes a dynamic and evolving entity, constantly adapting to the world around it. As we explore these new frontiers, the possibilities for creative expression are boundless, limited only by the imagination of those who dare to innovate.

6.4 REVITALIZING TRADITIONAL ART WITH AI

A world where the classical brushstrokes of the old masters meet the pixelated prowess of artificial intelligence is already upon us. This fusion is not a fantasy but a burgeoning reality with traditional artists embracing AI in their practices. Take, for instance, the painter who, armed with a palette and canvas, now also wields algorithms to breathe new life into classical painting techniques. By using AI, these artists reinterpret age-old methods, presenting them to modern audiences with a fresh perspective that retains the soul of the original while introducing a new layer of complexity. The algorithms act as a bridge, connecting the past with the present, transforming familiar scenes into revitalized masterpieces that speak to today's viewers. This harmonious blend of tradition and innovation allows artists to maintain their roots while exploring the vast potential AI offers, creating works that resonate across time.

Blending tradition with innovation, these artists navigate a fascinating landscape of hybrid art forms. Picture an artwork where AI-generated elements intermingle with traditional media. A canvas might feature AI-crafted patterns seamlessly integrated into a hand-painted scene, complementing each other. This approach invites a dialogue between the tangible and the digital, where brushstrokes meet bytes in a dance of creativity. The result is a new genre of art that challenges perceptions and pushes the boundaries of what's possible. Artists, once confined to the limits of their chosen medium, now have a plethora of tools at their disposal, allowing them to experiment and innovate in ways previously unimaginable. This fusion expands their creative repertoire and opens up new avenues for expression, offering a fresh take on familiar forms.

AI is proving to be an invaluable tool for artistic evolution, breathing new life into traditional art forms and keeping them relevant in the digital age. One of the most compelling examples of this is the digital restoration of classical works. AI technology has been employed to meticulously restore and preserve historical artworks, analyzing minute details to recreate colours and textures lost to time. This process involves training algorithms on existing pieces, teaching them to understand the nuances of an artist's style and technique. The restored works, while remaining true to the original, gain a new vibrancy, ensuring their survival for future generations. This application of AI not only preserves cultural heritage but also introduces these masterpieces to a new audience, fostering appreciation and understanding across generations. Through this digital preservation, AI is a guardian of our artistic legacy, safeguarding the past while paving the way for future innovation.

The impact of these pioneering efforts extends beyond the artworks themselves, inspiring future generations of artists to explore the fusion of AI and traditional techniques. Workshops and educational programs have sprung up, offering young artists the opportunity to learn how to integrate AI into their creative process. These initiatives empower artists to experiment with new tools and techniques, encouraging them to think critically and creatively about the intersection of art and technology. By fostering an environment of exploration and collaboration, these programs nurture the next wave of artists who will continue to push the boundaries of what is possible in the art world. The fusion of AI and traditional art is not just a trend; it is a movement that is reshaping the landscape of creativity, inviting artists to reimagine their practice in a world where technology and tradition coexist in harmony.

7 OVERCOMING CHALLENGES AND ADDRESSING CONCERNS

Picture yourself at the helm of a grand ship, navigating through uncharted waters, the horizon dotted with the promises of AI. Exciting, isn't it? Yet, beneath the waves lies the daunting prospect of complexity—algorithms, neural networks, and machine learning, all swirling in a sea of confusion. For many artists, stepping into the realm of AI feels like being tossed into the deep end without a lifeline. But fear not, for in this chapter, we will transform that turbulent sea into a serene lake where AI's mysteries are unraveled, and confidence is built one ripple at a time.

7.2 INTIMIDATED BY AI: BUILDING CONFIDENCE

Let's begin by unwrapping the enigma of AI, which I hope I've begun to do for you thus far. Imagine AI as a very competent sous-chef in the culinary art of creation. It doesn't take over the kitchen but assists in slicing through the tedious tasks, letting you focus on the main dish. At its heart, AI comprises algorithms, those little recipes that guide machines in learning and decision-making. When discussing machine learning, consider teaching your sous-chef to recognize ingredients by smell and taste. It learns from data, much like you learn from sketching countless faces until you can draw a portrait from memory. Understanding these concepts demystifies AI, making it less of a technological beast and more of a collaborative partner in your artistic journey.

Let's break down AI into bite-sized, digestible pieces to further ease the intimidation. Online resources like Coursera and Khan Academy offer beginner-friendly tutorials that walk you through AI concepts step-by-step. These platforms demystify the jargon, making it approachable for even the most tech-averse artists. Picture a comforting guide holding your hand as you explore this new terrain, ensuring you don't get lost in the labyrinth of complex algorithms. By engaging with these resources, you build a solid foundation, transforming AI from a daunting opponent into a familiar friend.

Building confidence with AI doesn't happen overnight; it's a gradual process akin to nurturing a delicate plant. Start with daily AI practice exercises and short bursts of exploration that familiarize you with AI tools. These exercises might include experimenting with a new filter or generating a simple pattern using an AI tool. Think of it as stretching before a workout, preparing your creative muscles for the innovation marathon. Over time, these small steps accumulate, reinforcing your understanding and confidence in using AI. It's akin to learning to ride a bicycle—wobbly at first, but with persistence, you soon glide effortlessly.

The journey from apprehension to mastery is often paved with the successes of those who have walked before you. Consider the stories of the artists we've discussed thus far who ventured into the world of AI with trepidation only to discover newfound creativity and expression. Take, for instance, a painter who began experimenting with AI to overcome a creative block. By integrating AI-generated patterns into their work, they found a fresh perspective and rekindled their passion for painting. These stories serve as beacons of hope, illuminating the path for others who may struggle with similar fears. Testimonials from peer artists resonate deeply, offering reassurance that the initial uncertainties of AI can indeed lead to a flourishing artistic practice.

Creating a supportive community is paramount in this journey. Engaging with forums and groups where artists share experiences and advice fosters a sense of belonging and encouragement. Platforms like Reddit and Discord serve as bustling hubs of discussion and collaboration where artists can connect, learn, and grow together. Imagine walking into a bustling café filled with fellow artists, each eager to share their AI adventures. By participating in these communities, you tap into a wealth of collective knowledge and support, transforming the solitary act of creation into a shared experience. These spaces offer guidance and camaraderie, empowering you to embrace AI confidently and enthusiastically.

Reflection Section: Building Your AI Confidence

Consider the following reflection prompts to help guide your journey with AI:

1. What AI concepts are you most eager to explore, and how can you break them down into manageable parts?

2. How can you incorporate daily AI exercises into your routine to build familiarity and confidence?

3. Who in your artistic community can you reach out to for support and shared learning experiences?

Use these reflections to chart your course, navigating the world of AI art with newfound assurance and curiosity.

7.3 BALANCING AI WITH TRADITIONAL TECHNIQUES

Imagine the thrill of discovering a new painting technique that breathes fresh life into your canvas, yet complements the time-honored methods you've cherished. This is the delicate dance of balancing AI with traditional art techniques. It's about finding that sweet spot where innovation meets tradition, allowing both to coexist and enhance one another. The key to this harmony lies in integrating AI into your established workflows without disrupting the essence of your artistic practice. Picture it as inviting a new band member to jam with your established group; they bring a new sound, but the melody remains distinctly yours.

Integrating AI into traditional workflows can be likened to incorporating a new instrument into an orchestra. It requires an understanding of each tool's strengths and how they can complement rather than compete. Take, for instance, the process of digital sketching. An artist might use AI to generate preliminary designs or suggest color palettes while still relying on their own hand for the final touches. This approach allows the artist to control the creative process, using AI as a guide rather than a dictator. By weaving AI into your workflow, you can enhance efficiency and open new creative avenues without sacrificing the personal touch that defines your art.

The human element in art is irreplaceable, a truth that remains steadfast even in the age of AI. While algorithms can mimic styles and generate patterns, they lack the emotional depth and intuition that only a human artist can bring. Consider a sculptor who uses AI to plan a complex piece, ensuring structural soundness and exploring potential designs. Yet, when it comes to the act of carving, it's the sculptor's hand that breathes life into the stone, imbuing it with emotion and intent. This blend of AI

precision and human artistry creates works that are both technically impressive and deeply personal.

In the world of hybrid art practices, several artists have successfully merged AI with traditional techniques, creating groundbreaking pieces that showcase the power of this synergy. One
such artist might use AI to generate abstract patterns, which they
then incorporate into hand-painted canvases, resulting in a
fusion of digital and traditional media. Another might employ
AI to design intricate textiles, weaving them into garments that
reflect technological advancement and ancestral craftsmanship.
These case studies highlight the potential of hybrid practices to
push the boundaries of creativity, offering a roadmap for those
eager to explore this intersection.

AI's role in the creative process is not to overshadow but to
enhance. Imagine an AI tool that assists a ceramicist in envisioning new forms and glaze combinations, offering suggestions
based on past successes. The ceramicist then uses these insights
to experiment in the studio, blending AI's analytical prowess
with their tactile skills. This partnership allows for greater experimentation and innovation, expanding the possibilities of what
can be achieved. By leveraging AI to complement traditional
skills, artists can maintain their unique voices while exploring
new territories of creativity.

Workshops and training programs offer valuable growth opportunities for those seeking to refine their skills in blending AI with
traditional art forms. These sessions provide hands-on experience with AI tools and demonstrate how they can be integrated
into various artistic practices. Participants might learn how to
use AI to enhance their painting techniques or how to apply
digital tools to traditional printmaking processes. Such workshops serve as a bridge between old and new, equipping artists
with the knowledge and confidence to incorporate AI into their
work without losing sight of their artistic roots.

Hybrid art technique workshops are particularly beneficial for artists looking to expand their repertoire. These programs focus on the intersection of digital and classical art forms, offering guidance on seamlessly blending the two. Participants might explore the use of AI to develop new painting methods or experiment with digital sculpting tools that complement their manual craftsmanship. By engaging in these workshops, artists can gain a more in-depth understanding of how AI can enrich their practice, fostering a spirit of innovation that respects and builds upon traditional techniques.

7.4 MANAGING RAPID TECHNOLOGICAL CHANGES

Imagine standing on the edge of a vast digital ocean, where each wave represents the latest advancement in AI technology. It's exhilarating yet overwhelming, especially when it feels like these waves are crashing in faster than you can keep up. Staying informed about AI developments can feel like trying to catch every drop in a downpour. The key is to equip yourself with an umbrella of strategies that keep you dry and informed. Subscribing to newsletters and publications focused on AI trends in the arts is one such strategy. Consider them your digital weather report, offering forecasts and insights into the ever-evolving landscape of AI. Reputable sources such as "AI Art Weekly" or "Creative Computing" provide a steady stream of updates, ensuring you remain on the cutting edge of AI advancements. By curating a selection of trusted newsletters, you can distill the deluge of information into manageable sips, keeping you informed without overwhelming your inbox.

In addition to newsletters, social media serves as a vibrant marketplace of ideas and innovations. Following key influencers in AI art on platforms like Twitter and Instagram can open doors to the latest breakthroughs and creative applications. These thought leaders often share their insights, experiments, and successes, offering a window into the dynamic world of AI creativity. By engaging with their content, you gain access to a community of forward-thinkers who are actively shaping the future of art. It's like having a backstage pass to the concert of technological innovation, where you can learn from the maestros of AI art. By staying connected to these influencers, you position yourself at the forefront of AI developments, ready to incorporate new ideas into your practice.

As we navigate this fast-paced digital landscape, adopting a life-long learning mindset is crucial. Think of it as a creative marathon, where the goal is not to sprint but to maintain a steady pace of growth and exploration. Embrace the idea that learning about AI is an ongoing process, one that evolves along-side the technology itself. Online courses offer a structured approach to this continuous education, providing regular updates on AI technologies and their applications in the arts. Platforms like Coursera, edX, and Skillshare host courses designed to deepen your understanding of AI, covering every-thing from basic concepts to advanced techniques. By enrolling in these programs, you can build a robust foundation of knowl-edge, equipping yourself with the skills needed to thrive in an AI-driven world.

The rapid pace of technological change can sometimes feel like a tidal wave, threatening to engulf even the most seasoned creatives. Managing this overwhelm requires a thoughtful approach, one that balances ambition with practicality. Setting realistic learning goals is essential in this endeavour. Rather than attempting to master every AI tool at once, focus on achievable objectives that align with your interests and needs. This might mean dedicating weekly time to explore a new software feature or setting a monthly goal to complete an online course. By breaking down your learning journey into manageable steps, you create a sense of progress and accomplishment, reducing the stress associated with rapid change.

In a world where information is abundant, tools that streamline updates are invaluable. AI news aggregators serve as a compass, guiding you through the vast sea of content and pointing you toward the most relevant developments. Platforms like Feedly or Flipboard consolidate AI-related content from various sources, curating articles, blogs, and reports into a single, easy-to-navigate interface. These aggregators allow you to tailor your information intake, focusing on topics that align with your creative goals and interests. By leveraging these tools, you can efficiently stay informed without being bogged down by the sheer volume of available information. It's like having a personal librarian, one who filters out the noise and delivers only the most pertinent insights, ensuring you remain at the forefront of AI advancements without feeling overwhelmed.

Embracing these strategies not only helps you navigate the ever-changing world of AI but also empowers you to integrate these technologies into your creative practice with confidence and foresight.

7.5 ADDRESSING AI MISALIGNMENT WITH ARTISTIC GOALS

As artists, we often find ourselves at a crossroads where our creative aspirations and the capabilities of AI tools don't quite line up. It's like trying to fit a square peg into a round hole. The first step to resolving this misalignment is to clearly define your personal artistic goals. Imagine your goals as a compass, guiding you through the vast landscape of creativity. Are you looking to explore new mediums, enhance your current style, or streamline your workflow? Setting clear objectives not only provides direction but also helps you evaluate whether the AI tools you choose align with your artistic vision. Participating in goal-setting workshops can be an invaluable experience in this regard. These workshops create a structured environment where you can reflect on your creative journey, identify your aspirations, and articulate them with clarity. By participating in these sessions, you gain a deeper understanding of what you truly want to achieve, laying a solid foundation for aligning AI tools with your vision.

Once your goals are defined, the next step is to evaluate the AI tools available to you. Not all tools are created equal, and selecting one that complements your unique style and objectives is crucial. Consider this process akin to an artist selecting a brush or a musician choosing an instrument. A checklist can be particularly helpful in this evaluation. Does the tool offer the functionality you need? Is it user-friendly, or will it require a steep learning curve? Can it integrate seamlessly into your existing workflow? By answering these questions, you ensure that the tool you choose will not only meet your current needs but also adapt as your artistic journey evolves. Remember, the right AI tool is one that feels like an extension of your creative self, enhancing your work without overshadowing it.

Sometimes, even the most advanced AI tools might not fit your needs right out of the box. This is where customization comes into play. Think of AI as a block of clay, ready to be moulded into a shape that suits your artistic style. Many AI tools offer settings and parameters that can be tweaked to better align with your creative vision. For instance, adjusting the algorithm's sensitivity or modifying its output parameters can drastically alter the results, making them more in tune with your personal style. This customization transforms AI from a generic tool into a personalized assistant, one that works in harmony with your creative instincts. By experimenting with these adjustments, you can unlock new dimensions of creativity, crafting work that is uniquely yours while benefiting from AI's capabilities.

Throughout the creative community, there are inspiring examples of artists who have successfully aligned AI with their artistic goals. Consider the case of a digital illustrator who used AI to generate intricate patterns that served as the backdrop for her hand-drawn characters. By customizing the AI's parameters, she created patterns that complemented her style, enhancing her work's depth and complexity. Similarly, a photographer might use AI to analyze lighting in their environment, adjusting settings to capture the perfect shot that matches their creative vision. These examples highlight the potential of AI to enhance rather than hinder artistic expression. These artists have expanded their creative horizons by aligning AI with their goals, producing work that resonates with their unique voice and vision.

Personal narratives from artists who have embraced AI provide valuable insights into this alignment process. One such story might involve a sculptor who struggled with visualizing large-scale installations. By integrating AI visualization tools into his practice, he could experiment with different designs and materials before committing to the final piece. This approach not only saved time and resources but also allowed him to explore creative possibilities that might have been overlooked. Another artist, a musician, could recount how she used AI to compose background harmonies, enriching her compositions while maintaining her signature sound. These narratives serve as testaments to the transformative power of AI when used thoughtfully and strategically. They remind us that aligning AI with our artistic goals is not just about technology; it's about embracing new ways to express our creativity.

The process of aligning AI with your artistic goals is a journey of discovery, experimentation, and growth. By setting clear objectives, evaluating tools, and customizing them to fit your needs, you can transform AI from a mere tool into a creative ally. This alignment opens up new avenues for exploration, allowing you to push the boundaries of your work and express your artistic vision in ways you never imagined possible. As you navigate this path, remember that the goal is not to replace your creativity with AI but to enhance it, using technology as a springboard for innovation. By embracing the potential of AI and aligning it with your goals, you can unlock a world of creative possibilities, forging a path that is uniquely yours.

8 FUTURE TRENDS AND INNOVATIONS IN AI ART

Picture this: you're at a bustling art fair, surrounded by the vibrant hum of creativity. A curious crowd gathers around a digital screen among the traditional canvases and sculptures. On it, a painting evolves in real-time, responding to the viewers' expressions and gestures. This isn't the work of a solitary genius locked away in a studio; it's the result of artists worldwide collaborating through AI-driven platforms. This scene isn't from a distant future; it's unfolding right now, showcasing the transformative power of AI in the art world.

AI's influence on artistic practices is nothing short of revolutionary. It's like handing artists a magic wand that doesn't just conjure images but reimagines the entire creative process. AI-driven platforms like Artbreeder and Google Jamboard are at the forefront, enabling real-time collaboration across borders. Artists can now co-create in virtual spaces, blending their unique styles seamlessly. These platforms offer integrated communication tools and version control, ensuring that creativity flows without the hiccups of traditional collaboration. By leveraging AI, artists can transcend geographical limitations, fostering a global dialogue that enriches their work with diverse perspectives.

Beyond collaboration, AI plays a crucial role in preserving cultural heritage. Imagine walking through a digital museum where ancient artifacts are brought to life through AI-powered restorations. Technologies like computer vision and natural language processing are helping to catalogue and restore price-less works of art, simulating original colours and textures that time has faded. This isn't just about preserving the past; it's about making history accessible to future generations. AI-driven applications also digitize ancient texts, enhancing readability and translation, allowing us to delve into the wisdom of bygone eras. In essence, AI acts as both a guardian and a storyteller, ensuring that our cultural heritage isn't just a relic of the past but a living narrative that continues to inspire.

AI's democratizing force in art creation is perhaps one of its most exciting prospects. By making sophisticated tools accessible to anyone with an internet connection, AI is levelling the playing field. Open-source platforms like Magenta and Runway ML invite artists of all skill levels to experiment with machine learning in their creative processes. These tools don't require a degree in computer science to use; they're designed to be intu-itive and user-friendly, fostering a culture of inclusivity and exploration. By removing barriers to entry, AI empowers a diverse array of voices to contribute to the evolving tapestry of art, ensuring that creativity is no longer confined to those with traditional training or resources.

As AI continues to evolve, new artistic mediums and forms are emerging, pushing the boundaries of what we consider art. Designed by AI algorithms, virtual reality (VR) art offers immer-sive experiences that transport viewers to fantastical realms. Artists like Memo Akten use AI to create VR experiences inspired by iconic works, inviting audiences to interact with art in unprecedented ways. These experiences aren't just visual; they engage multiple senses, creating a holistic encounter that blurs the line between the digital and the tangible. AI-generated VR art isn't just a new medium; it's a new way of experiencing art, one that challenges our perceptions and invites us to explore the infinite possibilities of the virtual world.

The influence of AI on global art trends is profound, fostering cross-cultural exchanges that were once the stuff of dreams. AI facilitates international collaborations, where artists from different corners of the globe come together to create something entirely new. These cross-border projects are more than just artistic endeavours; they're cultural dialogues that celebrate diversity and innovation. By using AI to bridge cultural gaps, artists can share their perspectives, techniques, and stories, enriching the global art scene with a tapestry of influences.

Reflection Section: Visualizing the Impact of AI on Art

Consider how AI might transform your artistic practice. Reflect on these questions:

1. How could AI-driven platforms enhance your collaboration with artists worldwide?

2. In what ways might AI democratize access to art tools and resources?

3. How can AI-generated VR art inspire new dimensions in your creative work?

Use these reflections to explore AI's potential in your art, considering how it might open new pathways for creativity and connection.

8.2 EMERGING AI TECHNOLOGIES FOR CREATIVES

In the ever-evolving tapestry of technology and creativity, new AI tools are emerging that promise to revolutionize the art world. Among these, neural rendering techniques are making waves. Imagine being able to render visuals so lifelike that they blur the line between reality and digital art. These advancements in rendering allow artists to create dynamic visual content with unprecedented realism. Whether it's a digital landscape that captures the subtle play of light and shadow or a portrait that seems to breathe, neural rendering elevates digital art to new heights. This technology enables artists to explore intricate details and complexities in their work, pushing the boundaries of what's possible. By utilizing these techniques, artists can produce works that captivate and engage, offering viewers an almost tangible experience.

AI's role in augmented and virtual reality is expanding rapidly, providing artists with innovative tools to enhance their creative processes. In the realm of VR, AI-enhanced sculpting tools are gaining traction, offering interactive 3D creation capabilities that were once the stuff of science fiction. Picture yourself sculpting in a virtual space, where each movement of your hand is translated into a digital form with precision and fluidity. These tools allow artists to experiment with shapes and forms in a way that traditional media simply can't match. The immediacy and responsiveness of AI in VR sculpting open up a world of possibilities, enabling creators to iterate quickly and explore new dimensions in their work. As these tools become more accessible, they are set to transform the creative landscape, making it easier for artists to realize their visions in immersive environments.

Interactive storytelling is another frontier where AI makes its mark, offering the potential to create personalized and adaptive narratives that respond to audience interaction. Narrative AI systems are designed to tailor story arcs based on the choices and reactions of the viewer, creating a dynamic storytelling experience that feels personal and engaging. Imagine a digital story that changes course depending on your decisions, offering a unique journey for each participant. These systems analyze user inputs and adjust the narrative accordingly, ensuring the story remains relevant and captivating. This level of customization allows for a deeper connection between the audience and the content, transforming storytelling into an interactive and immersive experience. By leveraging AI, creators can craft narratives that resonate on a personal level, drawing audiences into the world they've created.

The future of AI in music and sound design holds exciting possibilities, with emerging technologies poised to redefine how we create and experience sound. AI-driven generative music tools are at the forefront, enabling artists to compose complex soundscapes that respond to environmental inputs. Imagine a piece of music that evolves as you move through different spaces, adapting its tempo and melody to match the mood of the surroundings. These tools use algorithms to generate music that feels organic and alive, offering a new level of interactivity in sound design. By analyzing environmental cues, AI can create compositions that enhance the listener's experience, making music a dynamic part of the environment. This approach opens new creative avenues, allowing musicians and sound designers to craft immersive audio experiences that captivate and inspire.

As these emerging AI technologies continue to develop, they offer creative tools and opportunities that were once unimaginable. From neural rendering to interactive storytelling, these innovations are reshaping the landscape of art and design, inviting artists to explore new frontiers and push the limits of their creativity. With each advancement, AI is not only changing how we create but also how we experience and engage with art, making the future of creativity an exciting prospect filled with endless possibilities.

8.3 PREDICTING AI-DRIVEN ARTISTIC MOVEMENTS

In the ever-evolving landscape of art, predicting the future is both exhilarating and daunting. Yet, as AI continues to integrate itself into the creative process, we can anticipate a surge of artistic movements that blend technology with tradition. One such emerging trend is Techno-Organic Art, a genre that marries the precision of AI with the unpredictability of organic materials. Imagine a sculpture that breathes, its form dictated by algorithmic patterns but composed of living plants. Artists are starting to experiment with this fusion, using AI to orchestrate the growth and arrangement of natural elements, creating pieces that *evolve*. This harmonious blend of digital and organic not only challenges our perception of art but also prompts a reevaluation of our relationship with the natural world. It's a dance between machine logic and the chaotic beauty of life, offering a new perspective on the interconnectedness of all things.

As AI infiltrates the art world, it's set to inspire new styles and genres that push the boundaries of creativity. Consider Algorithmic Impressionism, a hypothetical movement where traditional impressionistic techniques meet algorithmic generation. Imagine a canvas where colours blend and swirl, capturing the fleeting essence of a moment, but with a twist—the patterns and shades are determined by AI based on environmental data or emotional cues. This fusion of past and future techniques could lead to works that are both familiar and novel, inviting viewers to experience art in a fresh, dynamic way. Artists working in this style might use AI to analyze light and shadow in real time, adjusting their brushstrokes accordingly. The result is a living painting, one that changes with the passing of clouds or the setting sun, embodying the transient beauty that Impressionists sought to capture.

The very way we experience art in exhibits is poised for transformation, thanks to AI. Imagine entering an art show where the pieces adapt based on your reactions. These Dynamic AI Curated Shows could use sensors and algorithms to gauge audience engagement, shifting displays to highlight works that resonate most. If a viewer lingers on a particular piece, the lighting might subtly change, or related artworks might appear, creating a tailored journey through the exhibit. This level of interactivity elevates the traditional gallery experience, making it more immersive and personal. As AI curates and adapts in real-time, it enhances visitor engagement and provides artists with valuable insights into how their work is perceived. This feedback loop can inform future creations, fostering a deeper connection between artists and their audiences.

Beyond aesthetics, AI-driven art movements hold cultural and social significance. Artistic creations have long served as commentaries on society, and AI offers new tools for these conversations. Consider artworks that use AI to address pressing societal issues, such as climate change or social justice. These pieces might analyze data patterns to visualize the impact of human activity on the environment or to highlight disparities in wealth and opportunity. By presenting complex issues visually, AI art can provoke dialogue and inspire action. This intersection of technology and commentary encourages viewers to reflect on their own roles within these narratives, fostering a sense of shared responsibility. In this way, AI art becomes a powerful medium for social change, challenging norms and inspiring collective introspection.

The cultural implications of AI art extend further, influencing how we perceive creativity and authorship. As machines become more involved in the creative process, questions arise about the nature of originality and the artist's role. Is a work less valuable if a machine assisted in its creation? Or does the collaboration between human and AI represent a new form of artistic expression? These questions don't have easy answers, but they do invite us to reconsider what it means to create. As AI-driven art movements gain traction, they will undoubtedly reshape our understanding of art, challenging us to embrace new paradigms and possibilities. In this evolving landscape, artists have the opportunity to redefine their craft, exploring the limitless potential of AI while remaining grounded in their unique visions and voices.

8.4 PREPARING FOR THE NEXT WAVE OF AI INNOVATION

Imagine yourself at the epicentre of a creative renaissance, where the brushstrokes of innovation are painted by algorithms and pixels. To thrive in this dynamic landscape, you must stay informed about the latest developments in AI technology. This isn't just about knowing what's new; it's about understanding how these advancements can be woven into your creative tapestry. Attending conferences like NeurIPS and SIGGRAPH can provide invaluable insights from industry leaders and pioneers. These events are treasure troves of knowledge, showcasing the cutting-edge of AI research and its applications in art. By participating in these gatherings, you gain access to a community of thinkers and creators who are shaping the future of creativity. You can network, exchange ideas, and even collaborate with others who share your passion for innovation.

Developing a skillset that is future-ready is crucial as AI continues to evolve and influence the creative sphere. This means more than just acquiring technical skills; it's about cultivating an adaptive mindset that embraces change and experimentation. You might consider enrolling in courses catering to artists interested in AI and machine learning. These educational opportunities teach you the basics of AI algorithms and how they can be applied to art. Some programs focus on practical applications, allowing you to experiment with AI tools and see firsthand how they can enhance your work. By building a solid foundation in these technologies, you're not just keeping pace with the industry; you're positioning yourself to lead it. You'll be prepared to explore new techniques, tackle complex projects, and continuously push the boundaries of your creativity.

In this ever-changing environment, building a resilient creative practice is essential. This involves adopting flexible and adaptive practices that allow you to evolve with technological changes. One effective approach is to engage in self-directed innovation projects. These are personal initiatives where you experiment with new AI tools and methodologies, testing their potential to enhance your artistic process. By setting aside time for these projects, you create a space for creativity to flourish without the pressure of external expectations. It's like having a sandbox where you can play, explore, and discover new possibilities. This practice keeps your skills sharp and encourages a mindset of continual learning and innovation. You'll become more comfortable with ambiguity and uncertainty, invaluable qualities in a rapidly advancing field like AI.

Networking and collaboration are equally important in staying ahead in the AI art world. Building connections with technologists and other artists opens doors to new opportunities and insights. Artist-technologist collaborations are particularly fruitful, as they bring together diverse expertise and perspectives. These partnerships often lead to groundbreaking projects that neither party could achieve alone. Consider the success stories of artists who have co-created innovative works with tech experts. These collaborations have resulted in installations that blend art and technology seamlessly, offering audiences unique and immersive experiences. By networking with professionals from different disciplines, you create a support system that fosters creativity and innovation. You can share resources, exchange ideas, and collaborate on projects that push the boundaries of what's possible in art.

As we explore the future of AI in art, it's clear that the landscape is rich with opportunity and potential. Staying informed, developing new skills, building resilience, and fostering collaboration are all strategies that equip you to navigate this exciting terrain. By embracing these approaches, you position yourself not just as a participant in this creative revolution but as a leader who shapes its direction. The next wave of AI innovation is on the horizon, and with the right preparation, you're ready to ride it to new heights of artistic expression.

9 TOOLS AND RESOURCES FOR AI-DRIVEN CREATIVITY

Imagine Leonardo da Vinci, armed with a digital tablet, fervently tapping away to create the Mona Lisa 2.0, aided by a chorus of AI-driven tools whispering suggestions into his ear. In today's world, the canvas is no longer limited by the dimensions of a wooden frame, nor is the palette constrained to the colours ground by hand. Instead, artists now have access to a myriad of AI tools that expand their creative horizons beyond the imaginable. These tools serve as digital muses, ready to assist, inspire, and even collaborate in creating masterpieces that blend human intuition with machine precision.

Navigating this digital realm can feel like sorting through a treasure trove of possibilities. To assist you on this artistic quest, I've curated a list of AI tools tailored for various creative disciplines, each offering unique features and benefits. Let's start with RunwayML, a versatile platform integrating AI into video, image, and sound projects. RunwayML's user-friendly interface makes it accessible to novices and seasoned creatives, allowing you to apply complex machine-learning models without extensive coding knowledge. Whether you're editing a short film, enhancing photographs, or mixing audio, RunwayML offers a seamless experience, enabling you to experiment with AI-driven effects and transformations that elevate your projects to new heights.

Artbreeder takes a different approach by fostering collaboration and creativity through its unique platform. This tool allows users to generate and modify art by blending images together, creating a dynamic space for artistic experimentation. Artbreeder is particularly powerful for those who enjoy the communal aspect of art creation, as it encourages users to build upon each other's work. By adjusting parameters and combining elements, you can produce entirely new artworks that reflect a fusion of styles and ideas. This collaborative ethos transforms the creative process into a shared adventure, inviting artists to explore the boundaries of traditional art forms.

The functionalities of these tools are indispensable for creative professionals looking to push their artistic limits. Take DeepArt, for instance, which uses AI-driven style transfer techniques to transform photos into stunning works of art. By applying the stylistic elements of renowned paintings to your images, DeepArt allows you to reinterpret your photographs with a touch of classical elegance. The process is akin to having your own digital art studio, where you can experiment with different styles and techniques without ever picking up a brush. This capability enhances your creative repertoire and opens up new avenues for artistic expression.

Similarly, Adobe Sensei stands out for its ability to automate design enhancements, boosting productivity and creativity. Integrated within Adobe's design software suite, Sensei leverages AI to streamline repetitive tasks such as image tagging, content-aware fills, and layout adjustments. By handling these tasks, Sensei frees up your time to focus on the more conceptual aspects of your work, allowing your creativity to flourish without the constraints of tedious manual processes. This tool acts as a digital assistant, offering intelligent suggestions and automations that enhance your workflow and elevate your art to its fullest potential.

When choosing the right AI tools for your creative endeavours, it's important to consider your specific needs and goals. For image editing, tools like DeepArt and Artbreeder offer unique capabilities, while RunwayML excels in multimedia projects that require a blend of video, audio, and imagery. If you focus on music production, platforms that leverage AI for sound design and composition might be more appropriate. You can select tools that align with your vision and enhance your creative process by assessing your artistic requirements.

Integrating these tools into your existing workflows can seem daunting, but it becomes a smooth transition with a few practical strategies. Start by identifying areas in your workflow that could benefit from automation or enhancement. For instance, if you spend considerable time manually adjusting photo edits, an AI tool like Adobe Sensei can automate these tasks, freeing you up to explore new creative ideas. Gradually introduce AI tools into your process, allowing yourself time to experiment and adapt. This approach ensures that the integration is seamless, enhancing your creativity without disrupting your established routines.

Tool Selection Checklist

1. Identify Your Medium: Determine whether your focus is on image editing, video production, sound design, or a combination. Select tools that cater to these specific needs.

2. Evaluate Features: Consider the functionalities each tool offers. Do they align with your creative goals? Are they user-friendly and accessible?

3. Assess Compatibility: Ensure the tools integrate smoothly with your existing software and hardware setup.

4. Experiment and Adapt: Allow yourself time to test different tools and find the ones that best complement your creative style and workflow.

9.2 ONLINE PLATFORMS AND COMMUNITIES FOR AI ARTISTS

Picture yourself stepping into a virtual gallery, an expansive digital space where creativity knows no bounds and innovation is the language spoken by all. Here, online platforms serve as the heartbeat of the AI art community, pulsating with ideas and collaborations that spark new forms of artistic expression. These platforms are the modern agora, where artists gather not only to showcase their works but to exchange wisdom and ignite collective creativity. One such vibrant hub is DeviantArt, renowned for its dedicated AI art community. This platform supports artists by providing specialized groups and forums where creators can share their AI-driven masterpieces and receive constructive feedback from peers. It's a supportive environment where novices and veterans alike can explore the potential of AI in art, learning from each other's experiences and insights. DeviantArt's AI community offers a wealth of resources and camaraderie, whether you're seeking inspiration, technical advice, or simply a space to connect with fellow creatives.

Another cornerstone in the digital art arena is Behance, a platform designed to showcase portfolios and connect with potential collaborators. Behance is an invaluable resource for AI artists, offering a stage to display AI-enhanced projects to a global audience. The platform's emphasis on visual storytelling allows artists to present their work in a compelling narrative, highlighting the intersection of technology and creativity. By curating a portfolio on Behance, you can attract attention from art enthusiasts and industry professionals and establish a network that can lead to exciting collaborations. This connectivity transforms Behance from a mere portfolio site into a dynamic community where ideas flow freely, and innovative partnerships are forged.

At the heart of these platforms lies the power of community engagement. Active participation in AI art forums is a gateway to learning and contribution, where artists can discuss techniques, share insights, and critique each other's work. Popular forums such as ArtStation, Reddit, and AIArtists.org serve as bustling marketplaces of ideas, each post a conversation that pushes the boundaries of what AI can achieve in art. Engaging in these forums nurtures a culture of continuous learning and collaboration, encouraging artists to challenge norms and explore the uncharted territories of their craft. By participating in community-driven art challenges, you can further foster creativity, pushing your abilities while gaining inspiration from fellow creatives who are equally passionate about the marriage of art and technology.

These platforms are not just about sharing and showcasing; they're vital networking tools. Savvy artists leverage these spaces to connect with peers, industry professionals, and potential clients, expanding their reach and influence in the art world. Social media plays a crucial role here, bridging the artist and a global audience. By developing effective networking strategies, you can engage with followers and collaborators on platforms like Instagram, Twitter, and LinkedIn, cultivating a professional network that supports your artistic ambitions. This engagement is not just about self-promotion; it's about building relationships that can lead to mentorship, partnerships, and opportunities that might otherwise remain out of reach.

The potential of these platforms extends beyond networking and community building—they're also treasure troves of collaborative resources that can enrich an artist's creative process. Many community members generously share tutorials, workshops, and educational materials, providing invaluable opportunities for growth and development. These shared resources offer insights into the latest AI tools and techniques, enabling artists to stay at the forefront of technological advancements in the art world. By accessing these tutorials and workshops, you can refine your skills, explore new methods, and deepen your understanding of how AI can enhance your work. Whether you're learning how to implement a new software tool or exploring innovative artistic techniques, these resources empower you to evolve and adapt in an ever-changing digital landscape.

9.3 EDUCATIONAL RESOURCES FOR MASTERING AI IN ART

In the ever-evolving landscape of art and technology, keeping your skills sharp and your knowledge current is crucial. Luckily, a treasure trove of educational resources is at your fingertips, ready to guide you through the intricate dance of AI and creativity. Let's start with comprehensive courses that take you from a curious novice to a confident creator. Coursera offers an AI Creative Work Specialization that's perfect for artists eager to incorporate AI into their work. This specialization covers everything from the basics of machine learning to advanced applications in art, providing a robust foundation that demystifies the complex algorithms behind AI-generated art. You'll find yourself exploring new dimensions of creativity, armed with the knowledge to make AI work for you.

Meanwhile, Skillshare hosts various classes focused on integrating AI tools into creative practices. These classes are designed with artists in mind, offering practical insights into how AI can enhance your artistic process. Whether you're interested in digital painting, music production, or graphic design, Skillshare's courses cover a wide range of topics, each focusing on hands-on learning. The platform's community-driven approach encourages collaboration and feedback, allowing you to learn from instructors and fellow students. This interactive learning environment fosters innovation and experimentation, essential to mastering AI in art.

For those who prefer more informal learning, YouTube is a goldmine of tutorials and workshops that provide hands-on experience with AI technologies in artistic contexts. Channels like "The Art of AI" and "AI for Artists" offer free tutorials on using AI tools, from basic introductions to advanced techniques. These videos are great for visual learners who benefit from seeing each step of the process demonstrated. They offer a way to learn at your own pace, allowing you to revisit concepts and techniques until you feel comfortable incorporating them into your own work. Local and online workshops also offer practical training in AI art creation, providing opportunities to engage with instructors and peers in real time. These workshops often include interactive sessions where you can apply what you've learned, gaining valuable feedback and insights that refine your skills.

Staying updated with AI trends is vital to remain at the cutting edge of technology and art. Subscribing to publications and newsletters focusing on AI developments in the arts ensures you're always in the loop. Blogs like "AI Art Weekly" and magazines such as "Creative AI" provide updates and insights into the latest trends, tools, and techniques. These resources offer a mixture of news, analysis, and case studies, helping you understand the broader context of AI in the art world. By keeping abreast of these trends, you can anticipate changes and opportunities in the field, positioning yourself as a forward-thinking creative ready to embrace the future.

The vast array of educational resources available today makes mastering AI in art more accessible than ever. From comprehensive courses to informal tutorials, there's something to suit every learning style and interest. Whether you're diving into a Coursera specialization, exploring Skillshare classes, or delving into the pages of a thought-provoking book, these resources equip you with the skills and knowledge needed to thrive in the intersection of technology and creativity. As you embark on this learning journey, you'll discover new ways to express your artistic vision, empowered by the limitless possibilities of AI.

9.4 FINANCIAL SUPPORT AND GRANTS FOR AI PROJECTS

Imagine you're an artist with a groundbreaking idea that could redefine the boundaries of AI in art, yet your financial resources are as thin as a starving artist's wallet. Fear not, for there is a world of financial support just waiting to be tapped into, specifically designed to nurture your creative endeavours. The journey to securing funding begins with identifying the right opportunities, and several organizations are dedicated to supporting AI-driven art projects. Creative Europe, for instance, offers grants that focus on innovative artistic endeavours where the lines between technology and creativity blur. Their support can be a game-changer, providing the resources needed to bring your visionary projects to life. Similarly, the National Endowment for the Arts (NEA) provides funding for projects that integrate AI and art, recognizing the transformative potential of this intersection. Their backing offers financial relief and lends credibility to your work, opening doors to further opportunities.

Once you've identified potential funding sources, crafting a compelling grant proposal is the next step. Think of your proposal as a persuasive narrative showcasing your project's artistic and technological merits. Begin with a clear and concise description of your idea, highlighting its innovative aspects and potential impact on the art world. Make sure to outline your project's objectives and methods, providing a detailed plan demonstrating feasibility and thoughtfulness. Remember, grant committees receive countless applications, so yours needs to stand out. Use visuals, such as sketches or mock-ups, to bring your concept to life and provide a tangible glimpse of your vision. Additionally, emphasize the collaborative elements of your project, showcasing how it will engage with the broader community or contribute to the field of AI art. By weaving a compelling story that aligns with the funder's mission, you increase your chances of securing the support you need.

While grants offer a traditional route to funding, crowdfunding has emerged as a powerful alternative for artists seeking to bring their AI-driven projects to fruition. Platforms like Kickstarter and Indiegogo provide a unique opportunity to reach a global audience, engaging potential backers who are passionate about supporting innovative art. When launching a crowdfunding campaign, crafting a captivating story that resonates with your target audience is crucial. Share your artistic journey, the challenges you've faced, and the potential impact of your project. Use engaging visuals and videos to communicate your vision effectively, and offer enticing rewards to incentivize contributions. By building a community around your project, you secure financial backing and create a network of supporters who are invested in your success.

Networking is another vital component of securing financial support for AI art projects. Building relationships with potential patrons, sponsors, and collaborators can open doors to funding opportunities and valuable partnerships. Attending art and technology conferences is a strategic way to connect with industry leaders, investors, and fellow artists who share your passion for AI. These events provide a platform to showcase your work, exchange ideas, and explore potential collaborations. Prepare an elevator pitch that succinctly communicates your project's vision and significance, and be ready to articulate your work's value in artistic and technological terms. By engaging with the community and fostering meaningful connections, you increase the likelihood of finding patrons who are eager to support your creative pursuits.

In the realm of AI art, financial support is not just about securing funds; it's about building a foundation for sustainable growth and innovation. You can turn your artistic dreams into reality by identifying the right opportunities, crafting compelling proposals, exploring alternative funding sources, and networking with key players. As you navigate this landscape, remember that each step forward is an investment in your creative journey, paving the way for future success and exploration.

10 SUSTAINING A CREATIVE CAREER WITH AI

I n a bustling city studio, the smell of fresh paint mingles with the hum of machines, where artists wield AI as adeptly as they do their brushes. It's an exhilarating time to be a creative. With AI, art isn't just about the finished piece; it's about the process, the story, and how we present it to the world. In this chapter, we'll explore how you can build a portfolio that showcases your skills and highlights your innovative use of AI. This isn't just about presenting artwork; it's about crafting a narrative that speaks to your unique vision as an artist in the digital age.

Building a portfolio with AI-enhanced art requires a keen eye for detail and storytelling. When showcasing your work, emphasize the unique AI techniques used in each piece. Whether it's a generative algorithm that developed a mesmerizing pattern or a neural network that inspired a colour palette, these details enrich your narrative. Highlighting these techniques demonstrates your technical prowess and invites viewers into your creative process. Consider crafting captions or short descriptions for each piece that explains how AI contributed to the final work, turning your portfolio into a dialogue between you and your audience.

Creating a cohesive portfolio narrative is essential to tying your AI-enhanced works together. Think of your portfolio as a novel, each piece a chapter in your artistic journey. Organize your work around central themes or concepts, such as "Nature and Machine" or "Urban Rhythms," to create a compelling story. This thematic approach captivates your audience and reinforces your personal brand as an artist. By weaving AI into your narrative, you can illustrate how technology and creativity coexist in your work, offering a fresh perspective that challenges traditional art norms.

Utilizing digital platforms for portfolio display is a strategic move to reach a broader audience. Websites like Behance and ArtStation offer dedicated spaces for artists to showcase their work, complete with features like project tagging and community engagement. These platforms allow you to present your AI-driven art in a professional and accessible manner, attracting potential collaborators and clients. Additionally, consider creating a personal website that integrates AI-powered tools for enhanced presentation, such as interactive galleries or AI-generated insights about your work. This not only elevates your online presence but also ensures that your portfolio remains dynamic and engaging.

Incorporating diverse media and formats into your portfolio demonstrates versatility and adaptability. Consider including video demonstrations that showcase your creative process, offering viewers a behind-the-scenes look at how you integrate AI into your work. These clips can highlight the evolution of a piece, from initial concept to final product, underscoring the transformative role of AI. By presenting a variety of media, you cater to different audience preferences, whether they're interested in still images, time-lapse videos, or interactive elements. This diversity enriches your portfolio and positions you as a forward-thinking artist ready to embrace the future of creativity.

10.2 MARKETING YOUR AI-DRIVEN CREATIONS

Marketing your AI-driven creations begins with understanding the diverse audience that appreciates and seeks out such innovative artwork. This means diving into market research to uncover trends and preferences within the AI art community. Start by identifying your audience—are they tech enthusiasts, art collectors, or perhaps both? Utilize digital tools and platforms to gather data on what kinds of AI art are gaining traction. Pay attention to trends on platforms like Etsy or Saatchi Art, where AI artworks are increasingly visible. Analyze which styles resonate most and consider how these insights align with your work. By understanding the market landscape, you can position your art to meet the desires of potential buyers, ensuring your creations find their way into the right hands.

Social media emerges as a powerful ally in amplifying your reach. Platforms like Instagram and TikTok are not just for sharing; they're vibrant communities where visual art thrives. On Instagram, use features like Stories and Reels to showcase your creative process, offering an inside look at how AI shapes your work. TikTok's algorithm, known for promoting engaging, short-form content, can catapult your AI art into viral success. A consistent posting schedule, engaging captions, and appropriate hashtags help increase visibility. Engage with your audience through comments and live sessions, creating a dialogue that builds your brand and deepens connections with followers. These platforms offer a stage where your art can shine, reaching audiences worldwide.

An engaging artist statement is crucial in communicating the unique blend of AI and creativity that defines your work. This statement should be more than just a biography; it's a narrative that weaves together your artistic journey, the role of AI in your creations, and the message you wish to convey. Use storytelling techniques to craft a narrative that resonates emotionally with your audience. Share anecdotes about your creative process, challenges overcome, and the inspiration behind your work. A compelling story not only captures the imagination but also offers a deeper understanding of your art's significance, encouraging viewers to connect with it personally.

Collaboration with influencers and galleries can significantly broaden your reach. Influencers specializing in technology and art can introduce your work to their followers, offering a platform that reaches beyond your immediate audience. Build partnerships based on shared values and mutual interests, ensuring your art is presented authentically. Additionally, engaging with galleries that appreciate AI-driven art opens doors to exhibitions and events where your work can be showcased to collectors and critics alike. These collaborations create opportunities for exposure and engagement, positioning your art within a broader cultural and commercial context.

10.3 NETWORKING AND COLLABORATING IN THE AI ART SPHERE

Imagine stepping into a room buzzing with creativity and innovation. Here, the future of art is being shaped. Networking within the AI art community is not just beneficial; it's crucial. By connecting with like-minded creatives, you open doors to endless possibilities. Attending events like NeurIPS and Ars Electronica can significantly enhance your career. These gatherings offer more than just speeches; they provide a platform to meet pioneers in the field, exchange ideas, and even forge new professional relationships. It's like a melting pot of creativity where technologists and artists unite, sparking inspiration and collaboration. Through these interactions, you can gain insights into emerging trends, discover new tools, and perhaps find your next project partner.

Collaboration is where the magic truly happens. The blending of diverse fields can lead to groundbreaking projects. Imagine a technologist specializing in AI algorithms teaming up with an artist known for their vibrant digital landscapes. Together, they create an interactive exhibition that responds to viewers' emotions in real time. Such tech-artist collaborations push the boundaries of what's possible, offering fresh perspectives and innovative solutions. These projects demonstrate that you can create something greater than the sum of its parts by combining skills. Exploring interdisciplinary collaborations enriches your work and broadens your creative horizons, making your art more dynamic and engaging.

The digital age has made engaging with online communities easier than ever. Forums and groups on platforms like Reddit and Discord are treasure troves of information and support. Here, you can exchange ideas, share resources, and seek advice from fellow artists and technologists. Active participation in these communities allows you to stay updated on the latest discussions and debates in the AI art world. Specific groups focused on AI art discussions provide a space to ask questions, share experiences, and even collaborate on projects. These virtual meeting places foster a sense of camaraderie, offering a supportive network that can be invaluable as you navigate the complexities of AI in art.

Seeking mentorship can be a game-changer in your artistic journey. Within the AI art community, experienced artists and technologists are often eager to share their knowledge and guide newcomers. Mentorship programs tailored for emerging AI artists connect you with those who have successfully navigated the field. These relationships can provide personalized advice, feedback, and encouragement, helping you refine your skills and approach. A mentor can offer insights into industry trends, introduce you to key contacts, and provide a sounding board for your ideas. Leveraging such opportunities accelerates your growth, equipping you with the tools and confidence needed to thrive in the AI art sphere.

10.4 CONTINUOUS LEARNING: STAYING RELEVANT WITH AI

Imagine AI as a fast-moving river of innovation, constantly reshaping the landscape of creativity. You need a sturdy paddle: continuous learning to keep your artistic canoe afloat. Embracing lifelong education is not merely a choice; it's a necessity in the ever-evolving world of AI. Platforms like Coursera and edX offer courses that cater to a range of skill levels, from beginner introductions to advanced AI applications in art. These courses allow you to learn independently, ensuring you can integrate new skills without overwhelming your schedule. Certifications from such platforms enhance your resume and keep your skills sharp and relevant.

Exploring new AI tools and techniques should feel like an adventure, not a chore. Dive into the unknown by participating in workshops and hackathons, which provide hands-on experience and foster a spirit of experimentation. These events are treasure troves of knowledge, offering insights into the latest AI technologies while connecting you with a community of like-minded creatives. By actively engaging in these opportunities, you can discover innovative ways to incorporate AI into your work, pushing your creative boundaries and staying ahead of industry trends. This proactive approach ensures that you remain at the cutting edge of artistic innovation.

Staying informed about industry trends is akin to having a compass in the dynamic world of AI art. Subscribing to AI art newsletters is a simple yet effective strategy to keep your finger on the pulse of the latest developments. These newsletters provide curated content, highlighting breakthroughs, emerging tools, and influential projects in the AI art sphere. By dedicating a few moments each week to digest these updates, you can maintain a well-rounded understanding of the field, ensuring that your work stays relevant and inspired by the latest trends and technologies.

Building a personal learning network transforms the solitary pursuit of knowledge into a shared endeavour. Forming peer learning groups and study sessions with fellow artists and technologists creates a collaborative environment where ideas can flourish. These groups offer a platform for discussing new tools, techniques, and concepts, fostering an atmosphere of mutual support and encouragement. By engaging in regular study sessions, you can deepen your understanding of AI while benefiting from your peers' diverse perspectives and experiences. This approach enriches your learning and strengthens your connections within the creative community, providing a solid foundation for ongoing growth and development.

10.5 LONG-TERM VISION: FUTURE-PROOFING YOUR CREATIVE PRACTICE

Imagine your creative career as a canvas, with each brushstroke representing a strategic choice that shapes your future. Developing a strategic career plan with AI involves setting both short-term and long-term goals. Begin by identifying achievable milestones that align with your artistic vision. Short-term goals might include mastering a new AI tool or completing a series of AI-enhanced artworks. Long-term objectives could focus on establishing a distinctive style or exhibiting AI art internationally. By setting clear, aspirational targets, you create a roadmap that guides your artistic journey, ensuring that each decision propels you closer to your ultimate aspirations.

Flexibility and adaptability are your best allies in this rapidly evolving landscape. Embrace change as an opportunity for growth, remaining open to emerging trends and technologies. As new art movements arise, consider how they might inform or enhance your work. For instance, the integration of AI with virtual reality is creating immersive experiences that redefine audience engagement. By staying attuned to these shifts, you can incorporate fresh ideas into your practice, keeping your art relevant and resonant. Being adaptable ensures your creative practice remains dynamic, allowing you to pivot and innovate as the art world evolves.

Aligning personal values with AI integration is crucial for maintaining authenticity in your work. Reflect on how AI aligns with your artistic principles, ensuring its use enhances rather than detracts from your creative intent. Consider ethical considerations as you plan for the long term. This might involve questioning the implications of AI-generated art on originality and authorship. By integrating ethics into your career strategy, you safeguard the integrity of your work, creating art that resonates with authenticity and respect for your creative values.

Investing in sustainable practices is paramount for ensuring the longevity of your creative career. As an artist, consider ways to minimize the environmental impact of your AI art. This might include using eco-friendly materials or optimizing digital processes to reduce energy consumption. By prioritizing sustainability, you contribute to a more responsible art community, paving the way for future generations of artists. Sustainable practices benefit the environment and enhance your reputation as a conscientious artist committed to making a positive impact through your work.

10.6 MONETIZING AI ART: OPPORTUNITIES AND CHALLENGES

The landscape of monetizing AI art is as diverse as exciting, offering creatives a palette of opportunities to explore. Traditional sales remain a solid avenue, with platforms like Etsy and

Saatchi Art allowing artists to showcase and sell their digital creations to a global audience. These platforms cater to various tastes and preferences, making them ideal for artists who wish to reach diverse collectors and enthusiasts. Selling AI art online combines the allure of handcrafted uniqueness with the accessibility of digital platforms, allowing you to connect with buyers who appreciate the innovative blend of technology and artistry. However, stepping into the world of online sales requires more than just showcasing your work; it demands an understanding of what captivates your audience and how best to present your art in a crowded marketplace.

Licensing and commissions offer another lucrative path, transforming your AI creations into versatile assets. Licensing your art for use in media, advertising, or merchandise can generate a steady income stream. This requires a strategic approach, ensuring that your work aligns with your partner's brand or project. Art licensing provides financial gain and expands your creations' reach, allowing them to resonate with wider audiences. Additionally, offering commissions can tailor your work to specific client needs, providing personalized creations that reflect their vision. Engaging in these ventures involves understanding market demand and effectively negotiating terms that honour the value of your artistic labour.

Navigating the challenges of monetization involves astute pricing strategies and market awareness. Pricing AI art can be complex, often requiring a balance between perceived value and market standards. Factors such as the piece's uniqueness, the time invested, and the intricacy of AI techniques used should influence your pricing decisions. Offering tiered pricing models or limited editions can create a sense of exclusivity and urgency, attracting collectors who value originality and rarity. Yet, setting competitive prices demands research and an understanding of what similar works command in the market, ensuring that your art is both accessible and appropriately valued.

Utilizing NFTs and blockchain technology introduces a modern dimension to digital art sales. Non-Fungible Tokens (NFTs) have revolutionized how digital art is bought and sold, offering a secure method of proving ownership and authenticity. Creating and selling NFTs involves minting your art on blockchain platforms and providing a digital certificate of ownership to buyers. This technology not only protects your work from unauthorized reproduction but also allows you to retain a share of future sales through smart contracts. Embracing NFTs requires a grasp of blockchain's intricacies and the ability to market your art effectively in this digital marketplace, but the potential rewards are significant.

10.7 FOSTERING A GROWTH MINDSET IN THE AI ERA

In the ever-evolving landscape of AI, a growth mindset becomes your compass. Embracing change and innovation isn't just an option; it's a necessity. Think of this mindset as the artist's palette, rich with colours yet to be explored. It requires you to cultivate curiosity and a willingness to experiment, akin to a scientist in a lab mixing chemicals to discover new reactions. Each new tool or technique opens up possibilities, serving as a catalyst for creative breakthroughs. Encouragement to explore these new ideas helps maintain a dynamic practice where curiosity fuels a continuous cycle of learning and discovery.

Fear of failure often looms like a shadow, but it can be a powerful teacher. When you view mistakes as stepping stones rather than stumbling blocks, each misstep becomes an opportunity for growth. Embrace the iterative process, where refinement and improvement are part of the journey. It's like sculpting a block of marble; each chip removed brings you closer to your masterpiece. By taking risks in your endeavours, you invite innovation and creativity, turning potential failures into valuable lessons. This mindset not only enriches your work but also strengthens your resolve.

Resilience is your shield against the inevitable setbacks that accompany innovation. Developing coping mechanisms is crucial to maintaining motivation. Consider strategies such as setting realistic goals, practicing mindfulness, and taking breaks to recharge. These techniques help manage stress, ensuring that challenges don't derail your progress. Like an athlete training for a marathon, building resilience prepares you to face obstacles with determination. This mental fortitude transforms setbacks into opportunities for growth, allowing you to continue your creative journey with confidence and tenacity.

Creating a supportive community fosters shared growth and collaboration. Encouraging peer support offers a network of like-minded individuals who can provide guidance, feedback, and encouragement. Collaborative learning environments, whether online or in-person, create spaces where ideas flourish and inno-vation thrives. These groups function much like a creative hive, where each member contributes to the collective knowledge, enhancing everyone's learning experience. By engaging with others, you gain valuable insights and contribute to a culture of creativity that inspires and uplifts. This sense of community nurtures a growth mindset, propelling you forward in the vibrant, ever-changing world of AI art.

10.8 EMBRACING THE UNKNOWN: THE ART OF ADAPTATION

In the ever-shifting landscape of creativity, uncertainty often feels like an uninvited guest. Yet, it is this very unpredictability that fuels innovation. As artists, embracing creative uncertainty can open doors to uncharted territories. Think of it as a blank canvas, where the lack of clarity invites exploration. This mindset shifts uncertainty from a source of anxiety to one of inspiration, encouraging you to experiment without fear of failure. Sometimes, the most profound artistic breakthroughs occur when you let go of preconceived notions and allow the creative process to unfold organically. By welcoming uncertainty, you transform it into a catalyst for growth, pushing the boundaries of what your art can achieve.

Developing adaptive strategies for change is crucial in navigating the unpredictable nature of art and technology. Scenario planning serves as a powerful tool in this endeavour. By envisioning multiple future scenarios, you prepare yourself for various possibilities, allowing you to pivot as circumstances evolve. This approach involves identifying potential changes in the artistic landscape and considering how they might impact your work. It's like rehearsing multiple endings to a play, ensuring you're ready for whatever the final act might bring. Scenario planning enhances your adaptability and empowers you to seize opportunities that arise from unexpected shifts.

Leveraging AI to enhance adaptability offers a technological edge in responding to creative challenges. AI tools designed for rapid prototyping and iteration facilitate quick adjustments to your work, enabling you to experiment with new ideas efficiently. These tools act as your digital studio assistant, helping you iterate on concepts without the constraints of traditional methods. Imagine having a collaborator that can instantly generate variations of your design, allowing you to explore different directions with ease. By incorporating AI into your workflow, you gain the flexibility to adapt swiftly, ensuring your art remains relevant and innovative in a constantly changing world.

Celebrating the journey of artistic evolution is just as important as achieving the final masterpiece. Reflecting on your personal and artistic growth allows you to appreciate the progress you've made, even when the path forward seems uncertain. Keeping a journal to document your experiences provides a valuable record of your development, highlighting the lessons learned along the way. This practice encourages self-awareness and fosters a deeper connection to your creative process. By acknowledging your evolution, you cultivate a sense of accomplishment that fuels further exploration, ensuring your artistic practice continues to thrive amidst the unknown.

CONCLUSION

As we reach the end of our exhilarating expedition into the world of AI-driven creativity, let's take a moment to reflect on what we've covered. From the fundamentals of AI to its myriad applications in art, music, writing, and beyond, we've explored a landscape as vast and varied as the human imagination itself. Each chapter has been a stepping stone on this transformative journey, equipping you with the knowledge and tools to harness the power of AI in your creative endeavours.

We began by demystifying the basics of AI and unravelling the intricacies of machine learning, neural networks, and generative models. Armed with this foundational understanding, we ventured into the realm of creative applications, witnessing firsthand how AI is revolutionizing how artists, musicians, and writers approach their craft. We discovered a world where technology and creativity intertwine in a captivating dance, from AI-assisted painting and music composition to AI-powered writing tools and interactive installations.

Yet, as with any powerful tool, we recognized the importance of wielding AI responsibly. Our exploration of ethical considerations sheds light on the challenges and opportunities that arise when machines become our creative collaborators. We grappled with questions of authorship, originality, and the role of human intuition in an AI-driven world, emerging with a renewed commitment to using these tools to uphold the integrity of our artistic vision.

Throughout this journey, my goal has been to empower you, the creative visionary, with the practical insights and strategies needed to future-proof your career and unlock new realms of artistic expression. By now, you've gained a robust toolkit of AI techniques, software, and platforms that can elevate your work to unprecedented heights. You've learned how to integrate AI seamlessly into your creative process, leveraging its strengths while preserving the unique essence of your human touch.

As you embark on the next phase of your AI-powered creative journey, I encourage you to apply these insights. Experiment with the tools and techniques we've explored, adapting them to your unique style and vision. Embrace the spirit of innovation and collaboration, seeking out opportunities to work with like-minded creatives and technologists who share your passion for pushing the boundaries of what's possible.

Remember, the world of AI is an ever-evolving landscape, brimming with possibilities yet to be discovered. As an artist in the digital age, your curiosity and willingness to learn will be your greatest assets. Stay informed about the latest advancements, attend workshops and conferences, and engage with the vibrant community of AI artists and enthusiasts. By remaining at the forefront of this exciting field, you'll be poised to seize new opportunities and make your mark on the future of creative expression.

As we close this chapter of our journey together, I want to express my heartfelt gratitude for your dedication, curiosity, and openness to embracing AI's transformative power. Your enthusiasm and creativity have been a constant source of inspiration, and I have no doubt that you will continue to create works that captivate, provoke, and inspire.

If you ever have questions or ideas or simply want to share your AI-powered creations, I invite you to contact me. This book may have ended, but our conversation is just beginning. Together, we can continue to explore AI's limitless potential in the arts, pushing the boundaries of what's possible and shaping the future of creativity itself.

So go forth, my fellow creatives, with the knowledge and tools you've gained. Embrace the unknown, for it is in the uncharted territories that true innovation thrives. Let your imagination soar, and let AI guide you as you craft works that leave an indelible mark on the world. The future of art is in your hands, and I can't wait to see the masterpieces you'll create.

KEEPING THE CREATIVE SPARK ALIVE

Now that you have the tools to harness AI and elevate your creative work, it's time to share your journey and help others discover the same possibilities.

Simply by leaving your honest opinion of this book on Amazon, you'll guide fellow artists, designers, and innovators toward the insights they need to blend creativity with AI technology.

Your review could be the spark that inspires someone to take their first step into this exciting world of AI-powered creativity.

Thank you for your help. Creativity stays alive when we share our knowledge – and you're helping me do just that.

Click here to leave your review on Amazon.

REFERENCES

- **The Influence of AI in Modern Art: Shaping Creative Frontiers** https://artplug.com/the-influence-of-ai-in-modern-art-shaping-creative-frontiers/
- **An Introduction to Generative Art: Examples ...** https://medium.com/@imhimanshu/an-introduction-to-generative-art-examples-artists-software-2a4627a36ff6
- **10 Must-Try AI Music Composition Tools for Modern ...** https://blog.empress.ac/10-must-try-ai-music-composition-tools-for-modern-musicians-clq2kjppz658041wr3nhbf8u6e
- **Neural style transfer | TensorFlow Core** https://www.tensorflow.org/tutorials/generative/style_transfer
- **AI and the Arts: How Machine Learning is Changing Creative ...** https://www.oii.ox.ac.uk/news-events/reports/ai-the-arts/
- **Harnessing GAN for Revolutionary Art and Design** https://www.cloudthat.com/resources/blog/harnessing-gan-for-revolutionary-art-and-design
- **AI and Creativity: The Rise of Neural Art and Music ...** https://medium.com/@neuralobserver/ai-and-creativity-8d1e6c381986
- **Neural style transfer** *(Wikipedia)* https://en.wikipedia.org/wiki/Neural_style_transfer
- **Top AI Tools for Creatives** https://www.designity.com/blog/top-ai-tools-for-creatives
- **A Simple Guide to Using Artbreeder AI | by Dira** https://medium.com/@bydira/a-simple-guide-to-using-artbreeder-ai-305471dd105c
- **2023 AI Music Generation Tool Comparisons | Restackio** https://www.restack.io/p/ai-music-generation-answer-2023-tool-comparisons-cat-ai
- **Best Practices For AI In Game Design 2024 | Restackio** https://www.restack.io/p/ai-in-gaming-answer-best-practices-2024-cat-ai
- **NAEA Position Statement on Use of Artificial Intelligence ...** https://www.arteducators.org/advocacy-policy/articles/1303-naea-position-statement-on-use-of-artificial-intelligence-ai-and-ai-generated-imagery-in-visual-arts-education
- **AI-Generated Content and Copyright Law: What We Know** https://builtin.com/artificial-intelligence/ai-copyright
- **Generative AI Has an Intellectual Property Problem** https://hbr.org/2023/04/generative-ai-has-an-intellectual-property-problem
- **Responsible AI: Key Principles and Best Practices** *(Atlassian)* https://www.atlassian.com/blog/artificial-intelligence/responsible-ai
- **Top 5 AI Art Generator Tools Of 2024 - Forbes** https://www.forbes.-

com/sites/technology/article/ai-art-generators/#:~:text=Some%20ex-
amples%20include%20Stable%20Diffusion,Deep%20Dream%20Gen-
erator%20and%20Dezgo

- **AI for graphic designers: 3 major benefits - Adobe Firefly** https://
www.adobe.com/products/firefly/discover/ai-for-graphic-
designers.html
- **12 AI Animation Tools to Enhance Your Creativity** https://octet.
design/journal/ai-animation-tools/
- **AI for Music Production: 10 Tools to Produce Like a Pro** *(Ditto Music)*
https://dittomusic.com/en/blog/ai-for-music-production-tools-for-
musicians
- **MARIO KLINGEMANN, art, data poisoning & ...** *(Clot Magazine)*
https://clotmag.com/interviews/mario-klingemann-exploring-the-
frontiers-of-ai-data-poisoning-ethical-challenges-art
- **Artist Sougwen Chung collaborates and paints ...** *(Washington Post)*
https://www.washingtonpost.com/business/2020/11/05/ai-artificial-
intelligence-art-sougwen-chung/
- **The Rise of AI in Film: How AI Script Writing is Changing the ...**
(Medium) https://medium.com/@channelasaservice/the-rise-of-ai-in-
film-how-ai-script-writing-is-changing-the-game-04509a15c9fe
- **The Next Rembrandt: Recreating the work of a master with AI**
(Microsoft News) https://news.microsoft.com/europe/features/next-
rembrandt/
- **AI-Generated Art: How Can Visual Artists Navigate This ...** *(Art
Marketing News)* https://artmarketingnews.com/ai-generated-art/
- **Challenges of AI in Traditional Art Techniques - LinkedIn** https://
www.linkedin.com/advice/0/what-challenges-blending-machine-
learning-yjiie
- **5 ways to help creative teams adapt to technological change** *(Agility
PR)* https://www.agilitypr.com/pr-news/public-relations/5-ways-to-
help-creative-teams-adapt-to-technological-change/
- **Embracing Creativity: How AI Can Enhance ...** *(NYU Emerging
Technologies Collaborative)* https://www.sps.nyu.edu/homepage/
emerging-technologies-collaborative/blog/2023/embracing-creativity-
how-ai-can-enhance-the-creative-process.html
- **Collaborative AI Systems for Art Creation | Restackio** https://www.
restack.io/p/collaborative-ai-systems-answer-art-platforms-cat-ai
- **AI in Art and Cultural Heritage Conservation - Ultralytics** https://
www.ultralytics.com/blog/ai-in-art-and-cultural-heritage-
conservation
- **41 Creative Tools to Generate AI Art** *(AI Artists)* https://aiartists.org/
ai-generated-art-tools
- **Artificial Intelligence in VR Art: A New Frontier** *(Artificial Paintings)*

https://artificialpaintings.com/blog/2024/06/11/artificial-intelligence-in-vr-art-a-new-frontier

- **15 Essential A.I Tools for Artists, Case Study and Reviews** *(Learn My Craft)* https://learnmycraft.com/15-essential-a-i-tools-for-artists/
- **Ai Art Collaboration Forums | Restackio** https://www.restack.io/p/ai-art-collaboration-answer-forums-cat-ai
- **What Is AI Art? How It Works and How to Create It** *(Coursera)* https://www.coursera.org/articles/what-is-ai-art
- **AI Grant** *(AI Grant Initiative)* http://aigrant.org/
- **AI and Digital Art Portfolios: A Comprehensive Guide** *(Artificial Paintings)* https://artificialpaintings.com/blog/2024/06/20/ai-and-digital-art-portfolios-a-comprehensive-guide/
- **How To Sell AI Art in 2024? | 10 Best Platforms To Sell AI Art** *(MonetizeBot)* https://monetizebot.ai/blogs/sell-ai-art
- **EAI ArtsIT 2024 – 13th EAI International Conference: ArtsIT ...** *(EAI Conferences)* https://artsit.eai-conferences.org/2024/
- **The Future of Digital Art: Trends to Watch in the Next Decade** *(Medium)* https://medium.com/@hilarion365/the-future-of-digital-art-trends-to-watch-in-the-next-decade-703a2aa98b57
- **Roberts-Islam, Brooke (2021, January 27)**. *"Zara Meets Netflix: The Fashion House Where AI Replaces Designers, Eliminating Overstock"* *(Forbes)* https://www.forbes.com/sites/brookerobertsislam/2021/01/27/zara-meets-netflix-the-fashion-house-where-ai-replaces-designers-eliminating-overstock
- **BrandXR**. *"AR Murals: Immersive Art Experiences"* https://www.brandxr.io/ar-murals
- **Augmented Island Studios**. *"The Journey: Interactive AR Mural"* https://augmentedislandstudios.com/augmented-reality-for/murals/
- **The Shorty Awards**. *"Warrior S3 Interactive AR Mural Experience"* https://shortyawards.com/16th/warrior-s3-interactive-ar-mural-experience
- **Norton Rose Fulbright – Copyright Protection for AI-Created Work** https://www.nortonrosefulbright.com/fr-ca/centre-du-savoir/publications/68947aaf/copyright-protection-for-ai-created-work?utm_source=chatgpt.com
- **Government of Canada / ISDE – Consultation Paper: Consultation on Copyright in the Age of Generative Artificial Intelligence** https://ised-isde.canada.ca/site/strategic-policy-sector/en/marketplace-framework-policy/consultation-paper-consultation-copyright-age-generative-artificial-intelligence?utm_source=chatgpt.com